Angels, Angels

Everywhere

Angels, Angels
Everywhere

DAWN MYERS

AN AVON CAMELOT BOOK

ANGELS, ANGELS EVERYWHERE is an original publication of Avon Books. This work has never before appeared in book form.

AVON BOOKS
A division of
The Hearst Corporation
1350 Avenue of the Americas
New York, New York 10019

Copyright © 1994 by Tamar Myers
Published by arrangement with the author
Library of Congress Catalog Card Number: 94-26038
ISBN: 0-380-77935-8
RL: 5.2

Library of Congress Cataloging in Publication Data:

Myers, Dawn,
  Angels, angels everywhere / Dawn Myers.
    p. cm.
1. Angels. 2. Guardian angels. I. Title.
BT966.5.M94 1994
235'.3—dc20

94-26038
CIP
AC

First Avon Camelot Printing: November 1994

CAMELOT TRADEMARK REG. U.S. PAT. OFF. AND IN OTHER COUNTRIES, MARCA REGISTRADA, HECHO EN U.S.A.

Printed in the U.S.A.

RA 10 9 8 7 6 5 4 3 2 1

To an angel named Blaney

Contents

Foreword

Angels are real. According to the Bible, they are special beings created by God, not ghosts or spirits of the dead. Angels are God's messengers and there are many stories in the Bible of their coming to earth to make special announcements. In some of these stories the angels make actual appearances, while in others they communicate through dreams. There are also many stories about angels sent to protect and guard people.

Angels are heavenly creatures in a class by themselves and have no permanent bodies. Although many pictures show angels having wings, they can take on any form they want in order to accomplish their missions. In fact, angels usually appear as ordinary people. There have even been cases in which angels appeared as animals. Since angels can be dressed in the latest styles and speak any language, it is quite possible to see an angel and not realize it.

Some people believe that everyone is assigned at least one guardian angel at birth. Many people claim to have seen their guardian angel, and my youngest daughter is one of these. She saw her guardian angel after she was critically hurt in a bicycle accident. Immediately following the accident she was unconscious and very near death. When she woke up in the hospital she saw her guardian angel sitting at the foot of her bed. What makes her story so believable is that there were two witnesses to this event.

Many people wonder why they never see their guardian angel. Perhaps they do see their angel, but don't realize it. Perhaps they hear their angel's voice from time to time, but refuse to listen. Whatever the reason, in most of the stories about angel encounters, angels are seen by people who are in serious trouble. Maybe serious trouble is what it takes to get people to see and hear what has been around them all along.

Following are ten stories of children whose guardian angels have been seen in action. The stories are all based on true events, although many of the details have been changed. Read the stories and decide for yourself what you believe about angels.

Jennifer's Angel

Blessed be the God of Shadrach, Meshach, and Abednego, for he sent his angel to deliver his trusting servants (from the flames).

—*Daniel 3:28*

Jennifer knew it was going to be the worst summer of her life. She didn't mind visiting Grandma Taylor, but staying with her for two whole weeks was far too long.

"Why *do* I have to stay that long?" she asked her mother, for what seemed like the millionth time.

"Because I have to go to Chicago for that job-training program. It's really important."

"But why can't I come with you?"

Mother sighed. "Because I can't afford it. I've already explained that. And even if I could, what would you do in a hotel room for two weeks?"

"Watch TV." Jennifer meant it. Watching TV in a hotel for two weeks would be much better than staying in Grandma Taylor's big old house. That place was almost

1

as big as a castle, and probably twice as spooky. Jennifer was sure it was haunted.

Mother shook her head. "I wouldn't feel right leaving you alone like that in a hotel room. I'll be taking classes until late every day. And besides, Grandma Taylor is feeling especially lonely this summer. Remember, it was only last July when Grandpa died. She could really use the company, you know."

"But she has other grandchildren to keep her company. What about Trisha? Or Matt?"

"Trisha is going to summer camp, and Matt is spending the summer with his other cousins in Arizona."

"That's great," said Jennifer. Under her breath she said, "Some people have all the luck. It just isn't fair."

Jennifer's parents were divorced. Jennifer had not seen her father since she was a baby. In fact, nobody had. After the divorce Jennifer's father went off to Alaska to drill for oil, and had not been heard from again. Grandma Taylor was her father's mother, and although she had always been a part of Jennifer's life, she wasn't Jennifer's favorite grandmother. That was Grandma Miller. Still, Jennifer thought she owed Grandma Taylor something. After all, Grandma Taylor was missing a son, just as Jennifer was missing a father.

Mother sighed again. "Of course, I could call Alison's mother and ask her if you can stay there."

"You will?"

"If that's what you really want. I'm sure your grandma will be happy to see you another time. But you would have been doing her a favor, you know."

It was Jennifer's turn to sigh. "No, leave the plans like they are. I'll stay with Grandma." No way was Mother going to make her feel guilty about not staying with

Grandma Taylor. After all, even Mother didn't seem to like Grandma Taylor all that much. "She smokes like a chimney," Mother once said, when she didn't know Jennifer could hear her. But it was true. Grandma Taylor always had a cigarette in her mouth. It made everything in her house stink.

"So it's settled then?" asked her mother. "You agree to stay with Grandma?"

"It's settled," said Jennifer. Under her breath she added, "But I'm going to have a terrible time, and my whole vacation is going to be ruined."

"Of course you can take Ariel and Sebastian with you."

"Of course," said Jennifer. Ariel and Sebastian were her pet goldfish. She had won them at the county fair the summer before and had managed to keep them alive almost a whole year. Jennifer was sure that had to be a record of some kind—or at least close to it.

There was still a week to go until her mother's trip, and all during that week Jennifer felt crabby. Even her best friend Alison couldn't cheer her up. After all, Alison was going to have two sleep-overs and a trip to the beach while Jennifer was gone. In the meantime all Jennifer was going to do was spend time with a smoky old lady in a creepy old house.

"At least I'm going to be doing Grandma a favor," Jennifer kept reminding herself. But it didn't help her mood any. Being nice to someone wasn't going to be nearly as much fun as a trip to the beach and two sleep-overs.

When the day came for Jennifer to go to Grandma Taylor's, she woke up with a pounding headache. "Great," she told herself. "I try to do something nice for somebody, and look what I get."

Even a pill didn't make Jennifer's headache go away. By the time her mother dropped her off at her grandmother's house, Jennifer's headache was so bad she thought her head might explode. She had tried to keep her mind off her headache by concentrating on the two fish that swam in the bowl she held in her lap. But even though the road had been smooth, the water in the bowl had sloshed around too much, and Jennifer had found herself getting queasy as well. Imagine getting seasick just from staring at a silly fishbowl!

"Jennifer!" said Grandma Taylor, who had come out of the house to meet the car. "I am so glad you decided to come!" The old woman hugged Jennifer so tightly that her ribs hurt. Fortunately Jennifer's mother had taken the fishbowl from her and was holding it.

"I'm glad to be here too, Grandma," said Jennifer, who could barely breathe. To herself she added, "Not!"

Grandma Taylor released Jennifer and took a step backward. "What have we here?" she said, pointing to the fishbowl.

Jennifer told her grandmother about winning the fish at the fair.

Grandma Taylor seemed surprised at first, and then pleased. "Well, I think I just might have a surprise for you." She hugged Jennifer again, and this time Jennifer could smell the smoke that clung to her grandmother's clothes.

Jennifer's mother handed the fishbowl back to her and unloaded the suitcase from the car, but she didn't stay long enough to come in. She had a plane to catch, she said.

As soon as Jennifer's mother had said good-bye, Grandma Taylor picked up the suitcase and headed back to the house. Jennifer had no choice but to follow after her, carrying the fishbowl.

4

The house was just as Jennifer remembered from her last visit—smoky and spooky.

"I'm giving you a new room this time," said her grandmother. Her voice was scratchy. "Just follow me."

Jennifer obediently followed her grandmother up a narrow wooden staircase that led to the second floor of the house. The first door on the left at the top of the stairs was her grandmother's room. The first door on the right was where Jennifer usually stayed when she visited. This time her grandmother led her down the long hallway to a room that was all the way at the end.

"This was your father's room when he was a little boy," said Grandma Taylor as she opened the door.

Jennifer looked around with interest. She didn't remember ever having been in that room before, which was not at all surprising. The Taylor house was not the kind of place Jennifer liked to explore. It was too easy to imagine skeletons in closets and secret trapdoors in the floors.

"I thought you might like to sleep in your father's old room. We hardly ever talk about him, you know."

Jennifer nodded. She was too busy looking around to answer. Her father's room was not what she had expected. Not that she had ever thought about it before. But if she had, she might have imagined it different. She certainly never would have imagined a room with wallpaper covered with fish designs. There were even fish on the bedspread and curtains. The lamp by the bed had an anchor for its base. On the wall next to the closet there was a round little door, which resembled a porthole on a ship. It was almost like being underwater, Jennifer decided.

"Well, what do you think?" asked Grandma Taylor.

"It's very interesting," said Jennifer, although actually

5

she thought the room looked kind of dumb. There were just *too* many fish.

"When I saw your fish I thought you might like it."

Grandma Taylor sounded a little bit sad, so Jennifer didn't bother to remind her that Ariel and Sebastian had names and weren't just any kind of fish.

"What do you want to do first?" asked Grandma Taylor when they were back downstairs. The bottoms of her teeth were very yellow and they reminded Jennifer of candy corn.

"We could see what's on TV," said Jennifer. Her headache had started to go away, and she was feeling better.

Her grandmother must not have heard her. She reached into a pocket of her dress and pulled out a battered deck of cards. "You always did like canasta."

Jennifer started to make a face, but stopped herself just in time. The truth was she hated canasta. It was Grandma Taylor who always insisted that they play the game. At least when Grandpa was alive, they had played rummy sometimes.

Without even asking Jennifer if she preferred another game, Grandma Taylor shoved some newspapers off the dining room table and began to deal out the cards. The visit was going to be worse than Jennifer had feared.

"Just a minute," Jennifer said. She ran back upstairs and retrieved Ariel and Sebastian and set their bowl on the table. If she was going to have to suffer playing canasta with Grandmother Taylor, so were they.

They played six games of canasta until it was time for supper. After tomato soup and grilled cheese sandwiches they played five more games. At last Grandma Taylor announced that it was time for bed.

For the first time she could remember Jennifer was actually happy to be going to bed. And she didn't even mind that it was upstairs in Grandma Taylor's big, spooky house.

Jennifer mumbled "good-night," and then, before Grandma Taylor could give her a hug, she scooted upstairs, leaving Ariel and Sebastian behind on the dining room table.

Jennifer was so happy to stop playing cards that she fell right to sleep. All the nighttime creaks and groans that big old houses have couldn't keep her awake. She didn't even dream. But then, sometime in the middle of the night, Jennifer woke up. It was her coughing that did it.

"This house really is smoky," she said to herself. Her eyes had begun to sting. This was something that had never happened to her before.

She got out of bed to open the window, and that's when she saw the smoke coming into the room under the door. The first thing she did was to touch the doorknob lightly with one finger to see if it was hot. The sudden burning pain made her jerk her hand back.

Jennifer knew about fire safety. She had learned about it in school, and her mother had gone over it with her many times at home. She knew that the right thing to do was to get down on the floor and crawl to the window. So at first she wasn't scared at all.

"Great," she said to herself as she crawled along the floor. "I try to do something nice for my grandmother, and now look what happens to me."

When Jennifer got to the window she found that it was stuck. Jennifer pushed up on the window as hard as she could, and just when she was about to give up the window came loose with a pop. From then on it slid up easily.

But Jennifer could still not get out of the window because a pair of heavy wooden shutters was in her way. No amount of pushing or pulling would open them. They had been nailed firmly shut.

I'm going to die, she thought. *I'm being punished be-*

cause I really didn't want to come and stay with Grandma.
Oh please, God, don't let me die.

Jennifer lay down on the floor and closed her eyes. She began to pray very hard. She prayed that God would send firemen to rescue her. She prayed that Grandma Taylor would be all right. And even though she thought it might be sacrilegious, she prayed for Ariel and Sebastian.

Suddenly she felt very calm and peaceful. She opened her eyes and looked around the room again. Maybe there was another way to get out. But by then the room was very smoky and it was hard to see. Jennifer strained to see through the cloud of smoke, but she could barely see the bed. The smoke stung, and Jennifer had to blink every few seconds in order to see anything at all.

Then suddenly Jennifer saw something she hadn't seen before and her heart began to pound with joy. There was a man in the room, and he looked like a fireman. Although it was too smoky to see his face clearly, Jennifer could see that he was wearing a fireman's hat and coat.

"I'm over here!" she called.

But the fireman didn't move. "There is a laundry chute over there on the closet wall," said the fireman. He had the kindest voice Jennifer had ever heard. "It's on your left. Crawl to it. The opening is just big enough for you. Slide down it and you'll end up in the laundry room. There's a door there that will take you straight outside."

Jennifer remembered seeing the funny-looking little door earlier that day—the one shaped like a ship's porthole—but she couldn't understand why the fireman didn't just pick her up and carry her out the way she had seen firemen do in movies. Maybe he didn't have time because of all the other things firemen did in movies, like chopping holes with axes and spraying water.

8

"What about my grandma? And Ariel and Sebastian?"

"They'll all be fine," the fireman said. There was something about his voice that made Jennifer believe him.

"Thank you," Jennifer said, and began to crawl toward the wall with the laundry chute.

"One more thing," the fireman said.

"Yes?" she asked without stopping.

"Love eventually returns to those who love."

Jennifer thought that was a stupid thing to say at a time like that, but she didn't dare say so. Instead she turned her head to look at him, but he was no longer there. All she could see was smoke.

Without wasting another second Jennifer crawled to the wall and squeezed her way through the little door. The laundry chute was made out of metal, and it was warm, but it didn't burn her. She landed in the laundry room, near the washing machine, on a big pile of clothes.

A few seconds more and she was out the back door and running around the house to look for Grandma's bedroom window. She hadn't gotten very far at all when she almost ran right into her grandmother, who was carrying the fishbowl.

"There you are!" cried Grandma Taylor, giving Jennifer another one of her bear hugs. Water sloshed all over Jennifer. "I'm so glad you're all right! I fell asleep downstairs, and I guess—well, the ashes from my cigarette caught the newspapers on fire. I tried to put it out, but I couldn't, and then suddenly the fire was between me and the stairs. I've been scared to death for you!"

Jennifer felt tears of happiness filling her eyes. "Oh Grandma, at first I was worried about *you!* But the fireman told me you would be okay."

"What fireman?" her grandmother asked. "I called

them as soon as I heard the smoke alarm, but they still haven't gotten here.''

"But they are here!'' insisted Jennifer. "At least one of them is. I saw him up in my father's room. He told me how to get out.''

Grandma Taylor shook her head. "Listen, Jennifer. You can just barely hear the fire trucks now. They're still blocks away.''

"But Grandma, I saw a fireman. He was wearing a fireman's hat. And he spoke to me.''

Grandma Taylor looked hard at Jennifer for a long time. "Then maybe it was an angel you saw,'' she said at last. "They do exist, you know. They are God's special messengers, and sometimes he sends them to show us the way.''

Jennifer could feel the hair on her arms stand up. "Grandma, do you think an angel can disappear, all at once?''

Her grandmother nodded. "I suppose angels can do anything they want. As long as it's God's will, of course.''

"Then it was an angel,'' agreed Jennifer. And suddenly she knew it was so. God had sent an angel to show her the way out of the burning house. And even better, the angel had shown her something else, something almost as important.

Without minding one bit, Jennifer gave her grandmother a big hug of her own.

Tara's Angel

For he orders his angels to protect you wherever you go . . . you can safely meet a lion or step on poisonous snakes, yes, even trample them beneath your feet.
—Psalms 91:11–13

Tara Neely hated snakes more than anything else in the whole world. The things she hated second most were alligators. Unfortunately the swamp near Tara's home in southern Georgia was full of snakes and alligators, so Tara stayed as far away from the swamp as she could. She wished that someone from the government would come and drain the swamp and build a beautiful shopping mall where the swamp had been. Of course that never happened.

But as much as Tara hated the swamp, and everything that was in it, she loved her daddy's stories about it. Daddy had been raised on the edge of the swamp, just like Tara, but unlike Tara, he had not been afraid to go into it. Daddy could tell swamp stories that would make your hair stand on end. Tara often wished that Daddy would tell stories about things besides the swamp, but he seldom did. Still, Daddy was such a good storyteller that if it had to be swamp stories or nothing, Tara would pick the swamp. But just barely.

One summer day Daddy, who worked as a postman, had trouble breathing. The doctor said that Daddy was suffering from something called stress, and that what he needed to do was to take off work for a couple of days and rest. Maybe even go fishing in the swamp.

"How about it?" Daddy asked at the supper table one evening. "Anyone want to go fishing with me tomorrow?"

Tara knew that Daddy meant her. After all, her two brothers were much younger than she. Andrew was only three, and Jake was still a tiny baby. As for Mama, she needed to stay home and nurse the baby.

"I promised Ginger that I would go over to her house tomorrow," said Tara quickly. That was sort of the truth. Tara had told Ginger that she would come over sometime that week, but she hadn't said "tomorrow" for sure. "But I could go fishing if you really wanted me to," she added.

"Oh, no, that's okay," Daddy said. "You go on over to Ginger's house."

Tara thought Daddy sounded disappointed, but she quickly put that out of her mind. There was no way Tara Neely was going to go into a swamp filled with snakes and alligators, even in a boat. She would do ten math problems, eat broccoli, or even sit next to smelly Ray Stevens in school rather than go into that creepy swamp.

But that night Tara had trouble sleeping. Twice she dreamed that Daddy was out in the swamp fishing when something bad happened to him and he needed her help. But just what the bad thing was that happened to him, Tara didn't know. After each of the dreams she woke up,

12

and as soon as she did the details faded immediately from her memory. Then Tara had a third dream. In this dream she met a talking bird who told her that if she went with Daddy on his fishing trip, he would be all right. After the third dream Tara could not go back to sleep, and the dream stayed with her, as clear as crystal.

Tara got up as soon as she heard Daddy moving about and surprised him in the kitchen. "I'd like to go fishing with you today, Daddy," she announced.

Daddy was delighted. He packed some extra sandwiches for Tara in the lunch kit and found an extra fishing pole. Then the two of them set off for the swamp just as the sun was rising.

Daddy's boat was tied up at a rickety wooden dock just at the edge of the swamp. It was a small metal craft that had a small engine attached at the rear, and had just enough power to move two people through the swamp. It definitely was not made for speed.

Tara watched Daddy prime the motor and then start it by pulling on a rope. But once the boat was headed into the swamp Tara closed her eyes. The swamp was filled with big trees, and from these trees hung grayish green plants called Spanish moss. The moss hung down from the trees like hundreds of beards, and helped to make the swamp spooky. The water of the swamp was as dark as cola and full of bubbles. Tara was sure that bubbles were caused by the snakes and alligators that lived in it.

Tara kept her eyes tightly closed until Daddy stopped the boat. She could feel warm sunshine on her and when she opened her eyes she saw that they were in an open area. The water was still dark and bubbly, but at least the trees with their mossy beards were no longer directly above them.

13

"This is the best place to fish this early in the morning," Daddy said happily. "Would you like me to bait your hook for you, kiddo?"

Tara smiled. She was happy that her daddy was so cheerful. Already the fishing trip made him seem more relaxed. The doctor had been right. All the medicine Daddy needed was this fishing trip.

The two of them fished for several hours. During that time Daddy caught seven big fish and four small ones. Tara caught only three fish, but one of hers was much bigger than any of the others caught that morning. Of course Tara let Daddy take the slimy fish off the hook for her.

"Why, that fish alone will be more than enough for supper tonight," Daddy said proudly.

Then suddenly Daddy clutched his chest. His face turned pale and large beads of sweat appeared on his forehead.

"I think it's my heart," he whispered. Then he slumped over and slid down into the boat.

At first Tara thought Daddy had fainted. "Daddy!" she shouted, as she dropped her pole and hurried to examine him. Then she saw that Daddy was barely breathing and knew that something very serious was wrong. Tara didn't know how to do CPR, but she found Daddy's pulse. It was very faint and seemed to come and go.

Tara closed her eyes tightly and began to pray with all her might. "Dear Jesus," she prayed, "please don't let my daddy die. Last night I dreamed that . . ." She stopped. Someone was calling her name.

Tara opened her eyes and glanced around. There was nothing to see but the open water and the big mossy trees on all sides. She closed her eyes and resumed her prayer.

Again Tara heard her name being called. This time she

did not open her eyes. "Who is it and what do you want?" she asked in a voice that was weak from fear.

"Don't be afraid, Tara," said the voice that called her name. Tara recognized it as the same voice that had belonged to the talking bird in her dream.

"Who are you?" Tara demanded.

She opened her eyes and looked around again. There weren't any birds to be seen—except for one very large bird perched on a moss-covered tree at the edge of the clearing. Tara had seen many kinds of birds near the swamp before, but never a bird this large, or one quite this color. This bird seemed almost as big as Tara. Although it was white, the sunshine reflecting off its feathers gave it a golden outline.

"Take your daddy home," said the bird in the distant tree.

"This is crazy," said Tara to herself. "Birds don't talk." She primed the little motor just as she had seen her father do. Then she pulled the cord. But nothing happened.

Then Tara pulled the cord over and over again, until her arms ached, but still she could not get the engine started. Exhausted, she began to cry.

"Get in the water and pull the boat," said the big white bird with the golden outline. Of course Tara didn't actually see the bird talk; it only seemed that way to her.

"I can't," Tara said. "There are snakes and alligators in that water." She said this to herself, not the bird, because she knew that the bird couldn't understand what she was saying.

"Get in the water and pull the boat over here," the bird seemed to say again. "Nothing bad will happen to you, Tara. I promise."

Tara looked over at her daddy. He was paler than ever, and he didn't appear to be breathing.

"Please, Jesus, help me," she said aloud, and she stuck a big toe into the water. Immediately the image of a huge alligator with snapping jaws flitted through her mind, and she yanked her foot back into the boat.

"Tara! You don't believe me, do you?" asked the bird. "I made you a promise, Tara. I keep my promises."

"But the water is horrible and nasty," cried Tara. "And it's full of snakes and alligators. I know it is, because Daddy is always telling me swamp stories."

Then it occurred to Tara that her daddy might never tell her another swamp story if she didn't get him out of the swamp and on his way to a doctor. "Oh please," she prayed. "I'm scared and I don't know what to do."

"Tara!" the bird called again. "Tara, Tara, Tara." Her name seemed to echo through the swamp.

Tara looked at Daddy again. He was as white as a sheet. She felt for his pulse, but couldn't find it. If Daddy was still alive, then his life depended on her. Closing her eyes, she climbed over the edge of the boat and slid into the black, bubbling water. In her hand she held the free end of a rope that was attached to the front of the boat.

The water was surprisingly warm. Mercifully her feet touched the bottom before the water got any higher than her chest. Muck oozed between Tara's toes, and she tried not to think about what she might bump into or step on. There was nothing else to do now but put one foot in front of the other.

In water that deep it was hard to walk fast. Tara tried swimming a couple of strokes while pulling the boat behind her, but a mouthful of the black water convinced her that walking was better. Fortunately the closer Tara got to the edge of the clearing, the shallower the water became. Finally the water came up only to her hips and walking was much easier.

But now she had a new problem. All the moss-covered trees looked the same. Without a compass (and Tara did not have one) it was going to be impossible to find her way back to the dock near her house.

"Please help me to find the way," she prayed.

"Over here, Tara!"

Tara looked up to see that the big white bird had flown to a new tree. She started to head in that direction, but then she saw what looked like a snake wiggling its way through the water between her and the bird. It seemed to be coming right at her.

Tara felt her legs begin to buckle under her with fear. "Oh please, God, save me," she prayed.

"Don't be afraid," the bird seemed to say.

Suddenly the snake, or whatever it was, turned and began to move out of Tara's way.

"Thank you, God," she remembered to say. And then she began to pull the boat just as fast as she could to the tree in which the white bird perched.

But each time Tara got close to the white bird, it spread its huge wings and flew away to land in a new tree. And each time it moved Tara would hurry after it as fast as she could. Then about the fifth or sixth time that the bird moved Tara noticed that the water was now only up to her knees. She looked ahead beyond the bird and saw some tall grass growing in the water, and knew that she was near the edge of the swamp.

"Oh thank you, thank you!" she cried.

For some reason this seemed to scare the big bird, for

quite suddenly he flew almost straight up from the tree he was perched in and disappeared behind a taller tree.

"And now what?" Although she knew she was near the swamp's edge, Tara still didn't know where to find Daddy's boat dock and the path that led up to the house.

But the bird was gone and there was no answer. Then Tara noticed a single white feather floating down toward the water ahead of her. She hurried to catch it before it landed in the swamp. It was by far the largest feather Tara had ever seen.

Tara stared at the feather in her hand in amazement, and then something even more wonderful caught her eye. Just a few yards away was Daddy's boat dock. The giant white bird had led her back home.

Later that day Tara learned that Daddy had suffered a heart attack. He didn't die; thanks to Tara, and the white bird, he had been rushed to the hospital just in time. It was a miracle, everyone said, that Tara had managed to find her way out of the swamp. In fact, it was a double miracle, Daddy said later, because there really were many poisonous snakes living in that swamp. And some big alligators too. All those stories had really been true.

But for Tara the real miracle was the big white bird. She knew now that it was not just a bird. She was sure that it had talked, for one thing—not the squawky mimicking sounds that parrots make, but real speech. And another thing, it didn't quite fly like a bird. Most birds flapped their wings when they flew, but this bird only soared.

When school began again in the fall Tara took the enormous feather with her and showed it to her science teacher.

"Hmm, that's odd," said Mr. Nelson.

"What's odd?" asked Tara.

Her teacher shook his head. "This feather doesn't belong to any of the birds that live around here. I've never seen anything quite like it. If you want, I can send it to some experts in Atlanta. Maybe they can tell us what it is.''

Tara smiled. She didn't need to send the feather to any experts to know what kind it was. She believed she had seen an angel in the swamp, and the angel had guided her safely back home. Even if the experts in Atlanta said that it was only a bird feather, Tara would always know differently.

Chris's Angel

The angel said, "I have come to stop you, because what you are doing is wrong."

—Numbers 22:32

It was the bottom of the ninth inning and the score was eight to six. The bases were loaded and it was Chris Newburg's turn to bat. Jimmy and Paul had struck out. Jason had walked, and Mark and Rob had each hit singles. Now it was up to Chris to bring them all in and win the game.

Chris walked nervously up to the plate, his favorite bat in his hands. It was the last game in the regional Little League championships and the stands were full. Chris tried to pick out his mother's face in the crowd again. At first he couldn't, then he saw her just where he expected to see her, in the second row of bleachers, right behind first base. She was wearing a bright red blouse, something she always wore to his games. She was waving to him, and he nodded back.

"Chris, Chris, Chris!" it seemed like the entire crowd was chanting.

When Chris stepped up to the plate his heart was pounding. "Oh please, Lord, let me be calm," he prayed. But the prayer didn't seem to work. When the pitcher wound up to deliver the first pitch, not only was Chris's heart still pounding, but his throat felt as though he had just swallowed hot sand.

Then the pitcher released the ball and Chris didn't have any more time to be nervous. The ball seemed to come shooting off the pitcher's mound like a rocket and all of Chris's attention was focused on it.

Chris thought the first pitch was high, and so he held back.

"Strike one!" the umpire cried.

The crowd roared its disapproval.

The second pitch came in at just the right level, but it was well outside.

"Ball one!" Chris thought the umpire sounded disappointed.

The third pitch was a curve ball and clearly too low, so again Chris let it go by.

"Strike two!"

The angry crowd roared again.

The fourth pitch was perfect. It came at Chris straight and even, headed right across the middle of the plate. With surprising calmness Chris swung the bat and hit the ball dead center. There was a loud crack and the ball soared over the head of the pitcher, over the head of the second baseman, and through the fingers of the outfielder. It didn't stop until it hit the fence.

The crowd stood and screamed for joy as the runners on all three bases came home. When Chris rounded third base and headed home, the crowd went absolutely crazy. Even the umpire's angry whistle didn't stop some of them from running out onto the field. Chris Newburg was a hero.

But Chris was not a hero to everyone. To everyone in Middleburg who loved baseball, Chris was a hero. To Mrs. Blanton, Chris's mother, he was a hero. To Dr. Blanton, Chris's stepfather, he was just a boy.

"I hate him," Chris said to his mother later that day. "I wish he were dead."

Mother looked shocked. "Why, Chris, that's an awful thing to say. You don't really mean that, do you?"

Chris felt his hands curl up into fists. "You bet I do. He didn't come to my big game, did he?"

"Well no, but your father *had* to work today. I thought you understood—"

"He's not my father!" Chris interrupted. "He's just your husband. My *real* father would have come if he could." Chris's parents had been divorced since he was three. The last time Chris had seen his father had been two Christmases ago. Since then there hadn't even been as much as a note telling them where he was.

"I'm sorry you feel that way about Bill," Mother said gently. "We've only been married a year. I'm sure if you'll just give him a chance, you'll learn to like him."

"I'll never like him as long as I live!"

"Chris, please," Mother said. "Let's not fight about this today. This is your big day, after all."

"*Was,*" said Chris angrily. "But now it's ruined because he didn't come to the game. And it's your fault for marrying him!"

"Doctors can't take the day off when their patients need them," Mother reminded him.

"Then you shouldn't have married a doctor. You should

22

have married a teacher like Jimmy's dad. He gets the whole summer off!''

''Bill tries to spend as much time with you as possible.'' His mother started to blink and Chris knew she was going to cry.

''Who cares?'' said Chris anyway. ''He hates sports, doesn't he?''

''Bill isn't crazy about baseball,'' she agreed. ''But he does let you watch all the sports you want on television.''

''Big deal.''

''Maybe you could show a little interest in something he likes.''

''Trains?'' Chris laughed. ''Trains are for little kids. For babies.'' Actually, Bill had a pretty net train setup in the basement. The mountains in his scenery reached all the way to the ceiling, and there were at least a dozen tunnels and bridges that his miniature ''N'' scale trains had to pass through and cross. It might even be fun to play with such a setup, if Bill would let him play with it *alone*. But Bill never let anyone touch his precious trains when he wasn't there. Not even Chris.

Mother wiped a tear from her eye with the corner of her apron. ''Chris, why do we have to fight about your father—I mean, Bill—all the time?''

''Because you were stupid and married him! That's why. Because you are so stupid.''

''Chris!'' It was Dr. Blanton, who had just walked into the room. ''How dare you speak to your mother like that?''

Chris turned his back and started to walk from the room.

''Freeze!'' Bill ordered.

Chris took one more step and then stopped. He was so angry that he could hardly see, and most of his anger came from the fact that he was afraid to disobey Bill.

"Apologize to your mother," Bill said.

"Sorry," Chris mumbled. He said it so softly that even a mouse in his shirt pocket wouldn't have heard it.

"That won't do," said Bill. "Apologize again so that she can hear you."

Chris tried to say his apology louder, but for some reason the words just couldn't come out. He opened and closed his mouth a couple of times, but that was all that happened.

"Chris, please, do what he says." Mother looked and sounded worried.

"Then go to your room," Bill ordered, "and stay there until you can apologize."

"Fine," said Chris. He stomped off to his room without looking back, and with each step he took he got madder and madder. The team was having a victory cookout at the coach's house that night. Everyone would be there, and of course they would all have lots of praise for the hero of the day. But unless he would apologize, he couldn't go, and because it was Bill who had ordered him to apologize, Chris knew that he just couldn't.

Chris got even more angry as the evening wore on, but he could not bring himself to leave his room and apologize to Mother. If he did that, then Bill would win. At least, that's what it seemed like to Chris. So Chris sat in his room and did nothing—nothing except think about all the fun he was missing by not being able to attend the coach's cookout.

Several times Chris heard the phone ring and he knew it was the coach, or his friends, calling to ask why he wasn't there. Chris could hear Bill talking on the phone a couple of those times, and although he couldn't hear what was being said, he could imagine it well enough. Chris decided that he hated his stepfather more than anyone he had ever met in his whole life, and that included Jerry Muncie at school, who had once given him a black eye.

At last the phone stopped ringing altogether and the house grew very silent. Chris guessed that his mother and stepfather had finally gone to bed. He waited almost another half hour, just to be sure, then, without making a sound, opened his door and stepped out into the hall. Everything was quiet, and there weren't any lights on except the night-light by the bathroom door.

Chris moved as silently as a shadow. He tiptoed down the hallway, across the living room, and down the basement stairs. It wasn't until he was in the basement and had shut the door behind him that Chris risked turning on the light. What he saw made him smile with satisfaction. There, spread out in front of him like a miniature world, was Bill's train setup. Now there was no one to stop him from playing with it, if that's what he wanted to do.

But Chris wasn't interested in playing with trains. Instead he headed straight for the garage. It took him only a few seconds to find one of his stepfather's hammers. "He'll be the sorry one now," he said to himself.

Chris hurried back into the train room. There was an excitement building up inside him. He could hardly wait to smash the train setup into smithereens. Even if Bill heard him, by the time he got downstairs there would be nothing left of his precious hobby.

"Take that!" he said aloud, and raised the hammer high above his head. He started to bring the hammer down on the train setup, but he couldn't budge it. It was as if the hammer was caught on something.

Chris turned his head and looked up. What he saw made his knees go weak. He let go of the hammer, but it didn't fall. That's because someone else already had a firm grip on it.

Chris spun around and then backed up against the train setup. His heart was pounding.

"Hello, Chris," said a tall, strange man.

"Who are you?" Chris tried to ask, but no sound came out. This time he had trouble speaking because he was so scared. The stranger seemed to know what he meant anyway.

"I guess you'd call me an angel," the man said. He was about the size and height of Dr. Blanton, but he was dressed in an umpire's uniform. There was even a silver whistle around his neck.

"Yeah, right," Chris said, and this time the sounds came out.

The stranger smiled a friendly smile. "I'm your guardian angel. Usually I try to stay out of things, but this time I couldn't. Of course I have a name," he added. "You can call me Ohrr."

Suddenly Chris no longer felt scared, but angry again. He hated surprises. He especially hated it when grown-ups interrupted his plans, and that's exactly what the stranger had done.

"What are you doing in my father's basement, Mr. Ohrr?" he demanded.

The stranger laughed, but it wasn't a mean laugh. "My name is just Ohrr. Angels aren't misters. But anyway, I thought Bill was only your stepfather, and not your father."

Chris jutted out his chin. "Yeah, that's right. So what? But this is his house, and you have no business being here."

The stranger smiled. "But I do have business being

here. Today was one of the happiest days of your life, Chris. It should stay that way. I came to stop you from making a serious mistake.''

''What mistake?'' Chris stared hard at the stranger, trying to recognize him. Maybe he was one of Bill's friends whom he had seen before.

''You were about to destroy your father's—I mean, your stepfather's—trains. You were doing it because you were angry, Chris. But destroying this''—the stranger pointed to the setup—''is not going to solve your problem.''

''I don't have a problem,'' Chris snapped. ''It's Bill who has a problem.''

The stranger shrugged. ''Deep down inside you're angry because your real father left when you were just a little boy. You felt abandoned. Is that right?''

''Maybe.''

''And then you got used to not having a father around, and now suddenly there is one. You don't feel like you need a father, do you, Chris?''

Chris shook his head. ''Well, maybe sometimes. I mean, it would be nice if Dr. Blanton—I mean, Bill—would come to some of my games.''

The stranger nodded. ''And he will, Chris. I promise you that. Just give him a little more time. Someday, soon, you and that man upstairs will be good friends.''

''I have enough friends,'' Chris said stubbornly.

''I know. But nobody can have too many friends, can they?''

Suddenly Chris felt very tired. His eyelids drooped. It had been a long day. All he wanted to do now was to crawl back to bed and sleep.

''Say, Ohrr,'' he said, ''if you don't mind—'' He

stopped. There was nobody in the basement but Chris. Even the hammer was nowhere to be seen.

Chris scratched his head a couple of times in confusion and then stumbled sleepily up the stairs and to bed. The rest of the night he slept like a hibernating bear. In fact he didn't wake up once until there was a knock on his door late in the morning.

"Come in," Chris called drowsily.

Bill stuck his head in the room. "Say, Chris, I've been giving it some thought. I've asked Dr. Green if he would handle my patients when your team goes to the state championships. I'd really like to watch you play. How does that sound to you?"

"Great," said Chris. He still didn't like the man his mother had married, and doubted if he ever would. But for now, he was glad that he hadn't destroyed the man's trains.

As for Ohrr, the angel, Chris decided to pretend that it had all been a dream. For the moment he would put it out of his mind. Someday, when the championships were over, he might think about it again. Maybe he would even ask Bill what he thought.

Jahmal's Angel

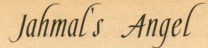

And there was war in heaven. Michael and his angels fought the dragon, and the dragon and his angels fought back.

—Revelation 12:7

Even with two pillows over his head Jahmal heard his parents fighting. They always fought. It had been that way ever since Jahmal could remember. Usually it seemed that the fights were started by his mother. She was always nagging Jahmal's father to get a job. But it takes two to fight, and Jahmal's father got angry when his wife nagged. Sometimes he even hit her. Once when that happened Jahmal jumped in front of his mother to protect her, but his father just picked him up and threw him across the room. Jahmal's head hit against a dresser and he had to have six stitches.

Tonight was Jahmal's birthday, but that didn't make a difference to his parents. They were at it again and didn't even seem to notice him—as long as he stayed out of the way.

"I don't care that you fought in the war," said Jahmal's mother. "I don't care if you fought in ten wars. Vietnam was a long time ago. That's no excuse for not getting a job now!"

His father got angry as usual. "You just don't get it, do you? The war messed me up. Here." He tapped his head with a finger. "I have such terrible nightmares that I can't sleep. How do you expect me to hold down a job?"

His mother didn't understand. "You look just fine to me. I think you're lazy, that's all. And don't talk to me about nightmares. Living with you is one big nightmare."

Jahmal's father got madder than Jahmal had ever seen him get before. He made a fist and started after his wife.

"Stay away from me, or I'll call the police!" Jahmal's mother screamed. She had threatened to do that many times, but she never did.

Her husband kept coming at her. Jahmal could see the veins on his father's neck bulge. That happened only when he was very angry.

"I'll call the police," Jahmal's mother screamed again. "This time I mean it!"

That night Jahmal decided to do it for her. He grabbed his jacket and ran outside before his parents could stop him. He didn't stop running until he reached the mini-mart two blocks away. Then, as soon as he caught his breath, he called the police, told them all about the fight, and gave them his address.

Then Jahmal started to walk. It was a cool evening and it felt good to be walking. Walking was a good way to burn off tension, and a way to kill time. Maybe the police would come and make his parents stop fighting, but even if they didn't, Jahmal did not want to go back home again for a long time.

In Washington, D.C., some of the streets are not safe to walk alone on at night, but Jahmal was too upset to care. He walked, without stopping, for almost two hours. A couple of times he saw some dangerous-looking men on the streets, but each time that happened he ducked into doorways and hid until they had passed. Once a car pulled up beside him and the driver tried to get Jahmal's attention. Then suddenly the car screeched away and went tearing around the corner and out of sight. Jahmal looked around but there was nothing to explain why the car had driven off so fast.

At first Jahmal didn't care where he was headed, but after about half an hour of walking he came up with a plan. He would walk to the Vietnam War Memorial, a special monument dedicated to the soldiers who died in the Vietnam War. The monument is made out of black marble, and it looks like a wall. On it are carved the names of thousands of dead soldiers.

Jahmal had never seen the monument, but he knew where it was. His father had been to see it and talked about it many times. "My name should be on it," his father said when he was depressed. "My best buddy's name is on it. Five people from my platoon are on it. But why not me? Why did I live, and they didn't?" Of course Jahmal could not answer a question like that.

It was after midnight by the time Jahmal got close to the Vietnam War Memorial. Except for a homeless man sleeping on the sidewalk a couple of blocks from the monument, there was no longer anyone out on the street. There was no moon that night and it was very dark near the monument, so Jahmal approached it nervously. Being there was spooky. And very sad. Moving slowly, he went right up to it and touched the cold, black marble. Then he began to run his fingers over the names that were carved into the stone.

"A whole lot of names, aren't there, son?"

Jahmal whirled around. There was a man standing there. He must have been a soldier because he was wearing battle fatigues.

"Who are you?" Jahmal demanded. He tensed himself to run. Not many people could catch Jahmal if he ran his fastest.

The soldier stretched out his hand as if he wanted Jahmal to shake it. Jahmal wisely refused.

"My name is Michael," said the man. "I'm an angel."

"No way," said Jahmal. He took a few steps to the side, just in case the man was crazy.

"Way," said the man.

Jahmal wasn't a fool. "Angels have wings. They don't wear fatigues. Where did you get those clothes, anyway? The thrift store?"

The man laughed. "No, these are special issue. Not all angels have wings, son. In fact, most of us don't. Most of us look just like you—or me." He laughed again.

"But we're African-American," said Jahmal. "I thought angels were white."

The man laughed again. "Angels don't have any color of their own. They can be whatever color they want to be."

"Prove it that you're an angel," said Jahmal. He meant it. If the weirdo in the uniform didn't prove who he was, Jahmal was going to make a run for it.

"Okay," said the man. "Let's see. Your name is Jahmal Sanders. You are twelve years old and about to finish the sixth grade. You live at 235 Ross Street, Apartment A. Your favorite food is macaroni with hot dogs and—oops, yesterday was your birthday, right? That's when you turned twelve."

"Today is my birthday," Jahmal corrected him.

Michael shook his head. "Nope, yesterday was. It's after midnight now, you know."

Jahmal didn't know what to think. "That doesn't prove anything," he said. "What are you, a spy or something?"

"No, just an angel. Well, the archangel to be exact."

"What's that mean?"

Michael scratched his chin as if he were thinking. "The archangel is sort of like a general, I guess. An angel general, of course."

Jahmal was hard to convince. "You still can't prove that you're an angel, can you?"

"Well, I know why you're here," said Michael patiently.

"Because I want to be," said Jahmal.

"That, and because your parents were fighting again tonight. Your dad has had a real hard time since he fought in the war, hasn't he? And, he takes it out on you and your mom, right?"

Jahmal nodded.

"Well, Jahmal, I'm here to tell you that everything will be all right now. When you called the police they came to your house and talked to your dad. One of them was a man who had been a soldier in Vietnam. He convinced your father to check into the Veterans' Hospital. The doctors there will take good care of your father. He'll be better in no time."

Jahmal stared at Michael. He was beginning to believe that Michael really was an angel. Or at least somebody with magical powers.

"I still don't get your clothes," said Jahmal. "Why would an angel dress like a soldier?"

Michael smiled. "I am a soldier. Think of me as the warrior angel. Of course it isn't people that I fight, but bad angels."

"There are bad angels?" Jahmal was surprised.

"Read your Bible," said Michael. "In the meantime we have to think about getting you back home."

"I could walk," said Jahmal. "That's how I got here."

Michael shook his head. "I know, but that's too dangerous. That guy in the car had a gun, and he would have used it. I had to shake him up a little to get him going."

"You were there? He took off because of you?"

Michael laughed. "I'd say he was pretty scared, wouldn't you? Anyway, I don't want you walking back. Let's find a telephone and you can call your mom."

"My mama doesn't have a car," Jahmal said.

Even though it was dark, Jahmal could see that Michael's eyes were twinkling. "I know, but your Uncle Joe does."

Jahmal's mother was very relieved to hear from him. She was also a little angry. "You had me worried sick, Jahmal. You know that?"

"Sorry, Mama," Jahmal said quickly. "Is everything all right?" He meant his father.

Jahmal's mother knew her son well. "Your father isn't here, Jahmal. Thank God, one of the policemen was able to talk him into checking into the Veterans' Hospital."

Jahmal glanced at Michael and saw him wink.

"Don't you move one foot from where you are," she said, after he'd told her his location. "I'm going to call your Uncle Joe and have him come right down there and pick you up. In the meantime, you be very careful."

"Don't worry, Mama," said Jahmal. "I'll be fine."

He turned his head to glance at Michael over his shoulder, but Michael wasn't there. In fact, Michael wasn't anywhere to be seen. Jahmal wanted to run back to the Vietnam War Memorial to see if Michael had gone back there, but instead he obeyed his mother and stayed by the phone. Fifteen minutes later his Uncle Joe showed up to take him home.

The next day Jahmal and his mother had a long talk. He told his mother about meeting Michael at the monument and what Michael had said.

"Well, doesn't that beat everything," his mother said.

"Do you think he was for real?" asked Jahmal. "Or do you think it was just my imagination?"

Jahmal's mother gave him a big hug. "All I know for sure is that when you left the house last night I started praying real hard. I prayed that the good Lord would send one of his angels to look after you. But I sure didn't expect him to send the Archangel Michael."

"I think your prayers were answered, Mama," Jahmal said. He truly believed that they were.

Caroline's Angel

See that you do not look down on one of these little ones. For I tell you that their angels in heaven always see the face of my Father in heaven.

—Matthew 18:10

Caroline was supposed to be watching her younger sister and brother while her mother was at the store, but she wasn't doing a very good job. That's because her best friend Dana had called on the phone with some interesting news.

"The new boy's name is David and he's twelve."

"What new boy?"

Dana sighed. "The new boy on my block, stupid. I told you there was a new family moving in down the street."

"Is he cute?" asked Caroline.

"He's rad," said Dana. "You should see him. He's helping his father move some boxes in now. Want to come over?"

"Can't," Caroline said. "I gotta sit for Alison and Troy. Mom's at the store."

"How long will she be gone?" Dana asked. "I mean, you could come over for just a minute, and get back before she gets home. She'll never know."

Just then six-year-old Alison came into the room. "Caroline—" she started to say.

"Go away," Caroline said. "Can't you see I'm on the phone? It's important business."

"But Troy is climbing that tree again," Alison said. Troy, who was only four, had recently discovered that climbing the maple in the backyard was loads of fun. The problem was, he wasn't supposed to climb it.

"Well, tell him to stop," Caroline said. She waved at her little sister to make her go, and then turned her attention back to the phone. "I'll bet he's already got a girlfriend," she said to Dana.

Dana laughed. "No way. He just moved in today. Come on, Caroline. It'll just take a minute. You can see him from our front porch. He won't even know you're there if you don't want him to."

"Okay, Dana, but just for a minute. And he'd better be cute."

"Trust me!" Dana said.

Caroline put the phone down and went to check herself in the mirror. She was pretty cute herself, she thought. Well, at least that's what her mother kept telling her. But so far none of the boys in her class seemed to notice her. Maybe this new boy—David—would be different. Of course if he was really cute, then all the girls in her class would like him. So it was important that Caroline got to see him first. As for Dana, she already had a boyfriend.

Dana lived only three streets away. Most of the houses between hers and Dana's had fences around them, but there were three that didn't. If Caroline cut through Mrs.

Greely's yard, and then through the two other unfenced yards, she could be at Dana's house in just a few minutes. Unless there was a problem.

The problem was Mrs. Greely, who didn't allow people to cut through her yard. If she caught you on her property, she yelled at you, and then told your parents. Mrs. Greely was crazy about wild birds, and she said that people cutting through her yard scared the birds away. Of course when Mrs. Greely yelled she scared even more birds away, but that didn't seem to matter to her. If Mrs. Greely was in her yard, Caroline knew that she would have to go around the block, and that would take a lot of extra time.

But good luck seemed to be with Caroline that morning. Mrs. Greely's car was gone, and there was nobody out in the yard. Caroline dashed across Mrs. Greely's perfect grass, and didn't stop running until she arrived at Dana's house. She made it in record time.

Caroline glanced up and down the street in both directions. There was no moving van to be seen. In fact, there wasn't anybody out at all, except for her and Dana.

"Where is he?" she asked between gasps.

Dana started laughing.

"Well?" demanded Caroline. "You told me to come right on over. Now where is he?"

"Fooled you, didn't I?" Dana laughed so hard that she had to hold her stomach.

"Very funny!" Caroline was not amused. She felt very silly and ashamed of herself. She and Dana often played tricks on each other, but this one was the best yet. She would have to think hard to come up with a way to pay Dana back.

Then suddenly Caroline remembered that she was supposed to be at home watching her little brother and sister.

Her mother might be home any minute, and she had risked being grounded all for nothing.

"Later!" she said and started to run back home the way she had come.

Unfortunately, Mrs. Greely had returned. When Caroline reached Mrs. Greely's backyard she saw the old woman's car parked in the driveway. And then she saw Mrs. Greely. She was headed right her way carrying a large bag of birdseed.

"Go around!" said Mrs. Greely crossly when she saw Caroline headed her way. "How can I make my yard a bird sanctuary when you keep trespassing?"

Caroline had no choice but to go past Mrs. Greely's house and around the rest of the block. All the other houses on that street had fences around them, and some of them had mean dogs inside the fences. "If Mrs. Greely wants people to stay out of her yard, then she should put a fence around it," Caroline said to herself.

Because she had to go around the block, Caroline was even later getting home than she had planned. Much to her relief, however, her mother had still not returned from the store. Just to be on the safe side—to make it look as though she had done a good job watching her sister and brother—Caroline headed straight for her backyard. Before she even got there she could hear her sister crying.

"Alison," she shouted, as she burst through the gate. She could see her little sister sitting alone on the back steps, but her brother was nowhere to be seen.

"Caroline!" Alison screamed when she saw her big sister. "Troy's in trouble!"

Caroline glanced around the yard again, but her little brother wasn't there. "Where is Troy?"

Alison pointed to the top of the large maple tree that was planted in the middle of the yard. "He's up there."

A very tired Caroline ran over to the tree. She looked up into its leafy branches, as far as she could see, but there was no sign of her brother.

"Alison," she called. "*Where* is he?"

Alison began to cry again. She continued to point to the tree.

Caroline moved out from underneath the tree's branches to where she could get a better look. At first she didn't see anything but green leaves. She squinted and held her hand above her eyes to ward off the sun. Finally she saw a speck of red, but it disappeared again as soon as she'd seen it.

She cupped her hands to her mouth. "Troy! Are you up there!"

There was no answer.

She called his name again. Then again. At last she heard a faint response. Her brother was up there. Just how he had managed to climb that high, Caroline had no idea. Four-year-olds were forever doing unexpected things, but climbing up to the top of a tree that was twice as high as the house had to be a record of some kind.

Caroline glanced at the ground surrounding the base of the tree. A lot of children's games had been played there, and the dirt was packed hard. If Troy fell even a little way, he could be seriously hurt. If he fell all the way from the top—Caroline couldn't bear to think of what might happen.

"Stay where you are! Don't move!" Caroline shouted. To Alison she said, "Run across the street and tell Mrs. Greely to call the police."

At first Alison didn't budge.

"Go!" Caroline shouted. Her little sister disappeared through the backyard gate.

"Dear God," Caroline prayed, "please let Troy get down from this tree okay. Please, God. It's my fault that he's up there."

Caroline's prayer would have been longer, but it was interrupted by the sound of a breaking branch, followed by the sound of something falling through the leafy branches, and finally a soft thud on the ground at her feet.

Caroline screamed and closed her eyes. She thought that she would faint. Then she heard what sounded like a giggle, and her eyes flew open.

"Troy?"

"Again," said Troy. He was holding his arms up in the air.

Caroline snatched her younger brother up in her arms, but he started to kick her. "Let me go!" he said. "Let me go!"

Caroline put him down and looked at him closely. "Troy, are you all right?"

Troy put his arms up in the air again. He seemed to be looking at something above him. Suddenly he put his arms down and made a face like he was about to cry.

"Tell the Christmas Lady to come back," he said.

"Who?" Caroline was afraid that Troy had hit his head. He wasn't acting at all normal—even for a four-year-old.

"Come back, Christmas Lady," Troy said. Then he started to cry.

The police arrived at the same time Caroline's mother returned. Troy was taken to the hospital where the doctors examined him thoroughly. They took X rays of all of his bones, even his head, but they didn't find any that were broken. Troy had somehow managed to survive a fall from the top of a thirty-foot-high tree without getting hurt. Even the doctors were puzzled.

"He probably fell only a few feet," one of the nurses said to Caroline's mother. "It's hard for children to judge distances accurately."

Caroline was furious. She had seen one of Troy's red sneakers near the *top* of the tree, not just a few feet from the ground. She whispered this to Alison.

"Maybe it was a cardinal," Alison said in a loud, clear voice.

The nurse smiled. Caroline felt like strangling both of them.

"I still can't believe you left Troy and Alison alone," Caroline's mother said when they were back home. "It's a miracle that Troy wasn't seriously hurt. Or even killed."

Troy heard his name mentioned and came into the room. "Troy want Christmas Lady to come back," he told them. "Troy like Christmas Lady."

"That's nice," Caroline said. She was glad for the interruption. Her mother had still not laid out the punishment, and Caroline was hoping to get off with just a warning.

"What Christmas Lady?" their mother asked.

Troy ran from the room. In a minute he was back with the angel that they put on top of the tree each Christmas. "Christmas Lady," he said matter-of-factly.

Caroline and her mother exchanged strange looks.

"Christmas Lady take me down from tree. It fun!" Troy giggled and ran from the room carrying the angel like a toy airplane.

Caroline and her mother sat speechless for a few minutes. "Well," said her mother at last, "I believe your brother says he was helped down out of that tree by an angel. What do you think of that?"

Caroline wasn't sure. She believed in God, but angels were harder to accept. "Sounds crazy," she said. "What do you think?"

Her mother shrugged. "I think it's always good to keep an open mind. Some people believe that angels only helped people back in Bible times. However, since then a lot of people have reported being helped by guardian angels. And a lot of those cases have involved little children."

Caroline went back outside and studied the tree that Troy had climbed. It was much higher than the telephone wires. She looked up to the spot where she had seen the flash of red that was Troy's sneaker. It wasn't possible for anyone to fall that far and not get hurt. It had to have been an angel who caught her little brother in its arms and gently laid him on the hard-packed ground.

But believing in angels seemed ridiculous! Especially in the nineties. Yet if it hadn't been for the angel—or whatever it was—Troy might well be dead. How much more proof did she need?

"Okay, so it was an angel," Caroline said to herself. "No big deal." As long as Dana and her other friends didn't know she believed in angels, it didn't matter one way or the other.

Just as Caroline was starting back into the house she heard her brother's happy giggles coming from the kitchen. She turned and waved at the treetop.

"Thank you," she said.

Eric's Angel

For the Angel of the Lord guards and rescues all who reverence Him.

—Psalms 34:7

It all began one Christmas morning when Eric Sorenson found a new pair of hockey skates under the Christmas tree. The skates weren't even wrapped, but they had Eric's name attached to them on a little card. Stuck on one of the skates was a big red bow.

"Thanks a million!" said Eric, giving each of his parents a big hug. Eric knew that his parents had bought the skates for him, and that it wasn't Santa Claus who had delivered them. Eric also knew that his parents didn't have much money, and that buying the skates had been a sacrifice for them.

"Merry Christmas," said Mom and Dad. They were pleased that the new skates made Eric so happy. He was a good son and they were very proud of him.

"I can't wait to try these out," Eric said. "I'm going to call Rob and Phil on the phone right now. Maybe we can get up a game of hockey."

The Sorensons lived on a farm and had their own pond. Some years the pond froze over by Thanksgiving and stayed frozen until March. But this had been an unusually warm year and the pond had only recently begun to freeze. The last time Eric's dad had checked, the ice on the pond was only two inches thick. That wasn't thick enough to support one skater safely, much less two hockey teams. Dad had a rule that the ice on the pond had to be six inches thick before Eric or anyone else was allowed to skate on it.

"I'll have to check the ice first," Dad said. "Last night was pretty cold, so maybe it is thick enough today after all."

"But first we're all going to church," Mom reminded them. "Today is Christmas. It's Jesus' birthday, and that is the reason we give presents. Now it's time for you to go upstairs and get dressed, Eric. The pond will still be there when we get back."

Eric sighed, but he obediently went upstairs to get dressed. *I don't mind going to church,* he thought, *but I really want to try out those skates. The sooner the better. After church tons of relatives are coming over for Christmas dinner, and I'm going to have to wait until they leave. And by then it might be dark. Too bad none of the cousins play ice hockey. In fact, only one of the cousins skates at all, Rebecca.*

Eric sighed again. He hoped it was loud enough for Mom to hear all the way downstairs. After all, he probably wouldn't get to try out his new skates until the next day— at least not in a hockey game. That thought made him unhappy, but there was nothing he could do about it.

On his way into the church Eric spotted Rob Anderson. He squeezed his way through the crowd to talk to him.

"Hey Rob," he whispered excitedly. "I got a brand new pair of hockey skates for Christmas. Want to come over for a game this afternoon?"

"Oh man," said Rob, "I'd love to. But we're going to my grandma's after church. Make it tomorrow?"

"Sure," said Eric, but he was becoming more unhappy.

Just then Phillip Aukrist, one of the best hockey players Eric knew, came in the door with his parents and little sister. Eric pushed his way over to see Phil.

"Hey, Phil, you want to play hockey this afternoon?"

Phil shook his head and then rolled his eyes upward. "I can't," he mumbled. "I'm grounded."

"On Christmas Day?" Eric asked. It was hard to believe such a thing could happen.

"Phil opened all his sister's presents too," explained Mrs. Aukrist. She sounded angry. "Now if you'll excuse us, we're going to go in and find a seat."

"Yeah," said Eric, and he felt more miserable than ever. If Rob and Phil, his two best friends, couldn't make it over for a game on Christmas, the chances were none of the rest of his friends could either. Eric went in and sat with his parents in their favorite pew near the front of the church, but he didn't even feel like joining in when his favorite Christmas carol was sung.

"Angels we have heard on high," the congregation began to sing, but Eric kept his mouth tightly closed. Even when they got to the part that went "Glo-----------ria," Eric refused to sing. Mrs. Sorenson looked at her son in surprise. Usually he sang that part so loudly that the people in the row in front of them turned around and stared.

After church Eric helped his mother get ready for the guests, but he was still crabby. He must have sighed a million times, but Mom didn't seem to notice. Meanwhile

Dad went outside to check on the farm animals. He was gone much longer than usual.

"It wouldn't have been safe to skate today, anyway," he said when he came back in. "I just checked the ice in three places. It must not have gotten as cold as I thought. The ice is still only two inches thick. In fact, in some places it's even thinner than that."

Eric felt even worse. Now there was no possibility of his trying the new skates that day. Even by himself. He almost wished that his parents had given him something else for Christmas. After all, he had an old pair of skates, and although they no longer fit so well, if he scrunched up his toes they weren't so bad. If his parents had given him something else, like maybe a Walkman with dual cassettes, at least he could have enjoyed Christmas.

Things got even worse when his cousin Rebecca arrived. "I brought my skates," she announced as she came in the door. "How long is it until we eat?"

Everyone laughed, except Eric. "Rebecca, honey," Dad said, "there isn't going to be any skating today. The ice on the pond isn't thick enough."

"Rats," said Rebecca, and then she went off to examine the Christmas tree. She didn't even seem to be upset at the bad news.

That's because she's just a girl, Eric told himself. *All she has is figure skates. If she played hockey and had a new pair of hockey skates, then she'd understand.*

Unfortunately, Rebecca was the only cousin there that year who was at all near Eric's age. The others were all babies, or, worse yet, preschoolers. Kids that age couldn't play anything worthwhile. All they could do was get on your nerves.

The Sorensons and their relatives ate Christmas dinner

in the middle of the afternoon. As soon as the meal was over, Eric, who had hardly eaten anything, went outside to be by himself. At first he wandered over to the barn to see how the cows were doing. They were doing just fine, thank you, and, except for a couple of moos, they didn't have any bright ideas about how to make his day go better. They just munched on their hay and switched their tails back and forth. They certainly weren't any fun to be around. Even Rebecca was more interesting than a cow, Eric decided.

Finally Eric got bored and was on his way back to the house when he had a bright idea. Without wasting any time, and taking great care not to make any noise, he sneaked into his room using the back outside stairs. A few minutes later he had his brand-new skates in his hands and was headed for the pond.

The Sorenson's pond was a long way from the house, and you couldn't see it all from there. It took Eric at least five minutes to get to the pond, but it was worth the trip. When Eric got there he could see that Dad was wrong. The ice looked plenty thick. Eric was sure that he had skated on ice just like that many times before. Just to be on the safe side, Eric walked carefully out onto the ice for several feet. Nothing happened. Cautiously, Eric jumped up and down twice. Again, nothing happened. Then Eric jumped up and down many times, with all his might, but still the ice held.

The worst thing was that Eric thought he heard a soft creaking sound, but that was only when he was jumping his hardest. Satisfied, Eric sat down on a log and put on his new skates. They were wonderful. The boot part fit perfectly—there was even some room to grow. The blades on the new skates were much sharper than the blades on his old skates, which meant that Eric could skate even faster than he used to.

Eric stepped out onto the ice in his new skates and then glided out into the middle of the pond. The new skates moved so smoothly that Eric felt as if he was flying. It would be a cinch to beat any of his friends in a skating race now, and when it came to that hockey game—well, Eric would mop up the ice with those new skates.

For several minutes Eric skated around and around in big circles, and then he tried some real sharp turns, just like the ones he would have to make in a hockey game. Then suddenly, without any warning, there was a sharp crack. The ice under Eric's feet gave way, and he plunged into the frigid water. It seemed as if he went down, down almost to the bottom. He had to swim his hardest just to get back to the surface.

Eric gasped for air. It felt as though someone was stabbing his lungs. He grabbed for the edge of the ice, but missed. Already his body had started to go numb with cold, and his fingers were as stiff as boards. Eric lunged for the ice again. Again he missed.

It was almost impossible to move at all because of the cold, and the heavy wet clothes and heavy skates that were dragging him down. *I'm going to die,* Eric thought, as he realized that he was sinking again. *I'm going to die because I couldn't wait to try out some silly skates.*

"Oh please, God," Eric prayed, "help me. I don't deserve your help, but I don't want to drown. Please help me."

The next thing Eric remembered clearly was waking up in a hospital bed. His parents stood on either side of him. Mom was crying softly.

"Welcome back, son," Dad said.

"Dad," was all Eric could say. His throat burned.

Dad smiled. "It's okay, you don't need to talk. You're in County Hospital, and Mom and I are both here. That's all that matters."

Eric drifted back to sleep. When he awoke again he felt much better and was able to talk with his parents.

"Who saved me?" was the first thing he asked.

Mom and Dad exchanged glances. "Maybe Rebecca should tell you," Mom said at last. "She saw it all."

Rebecca had been waiting outside and was eager to fill Eric in. "I was bored too," she said, "so I decided to make a game out of following you."

Eric smiled. "I hope it was fun."

Rebecca made a face. "Not at first. Who wants to sit around and look at cows all day? Anyway, I saw you sneak up the back stairs and get your skates. So, I followed you to the pond and hid behind some bushes. I saw the whole thing. You crashing through the ice—everything."

Eric stared at her in astonishment. *"You* pulled me out?"

Rebecca shook her head. "I was afraid I'd fall in too. I started to run for help, but something made me turn and look behind me. That's when I saw him."

"Him?"

She nodded. "Actually, I couldn't tell if it was a man or a woman. Their clothes were white and they sort of blended in with the snow. Anyway, whoever it was reached down into the water and pulled you out. Then they carried you to the shore and laid you on a snowbank."

Eric sat up. "Well, who was it?"

Rebecca shrugged. "Beats me. I started to run over to you, but the stranger disappeared."

"You mean he just vanished? Like into thin air." It was hard not to be sarcastic.

"Exactly." Rebecca turned to Eric's father. "You tell him the rest," she said.

"Well," Dad began, "after the stranger vanished, Rebecca ran and got us, and of course we called the ambulance right away. Mom waited at the house for the ambulance, but I went straight to the pond. When I got there, you were lying on a snowbank about ten feet from the pond." Dad paused and looked at Mom.

"What is it?" Eric asked. "What's all the mystery?"

"There weren't any footprints near you," Dad said.

"That's right," Rebecca chimed in. "The only footprints near the pond were yours, but there weren't any footprints at all leading to the snowbank."

"I've heard of things like this before," Mom said, "but I never quite believed them."

Eric stared at his mother. "Believed what?" he asked.

"Angels," Dad said. "Your mother and I think that can be the only explanation."

"You mean it was an angel who pulled me from the pond?"

All three visitors nodded.

Eric felt himself getting goose bumps, but he wasn't cold. In addition to the skates, he had been given a very special gift for Christmas. His life had been saved by his guardian angel.

Ramala's Angel

"My God has sent his angel," he said, "to shut the lions' mouths so that they can't touch me."
                                        —*Daniel 6:22*

The forest that bordered Kamala's village was home to tigers and rhinoceroses and many kinds of poisonous snakes. The villagers, mostly women and children, were usually safe as long as they stayed out of the forest. The village men had gone to the big cities to look for work, and Kamala's father was one of them.

Although Kamala lived on the edge of the forest, she never saw a wild tiger until the day she walked through the forest to get a doctor for her very sick brother. The tiger Kamala saw was a man-eater which had already killed and eaten two people. He might have eaten Kamala, too, had it not been for the angel that came to shut his mouth.

One morning Kamala's baby brother Prem woke up crying. Their mother felt his forehead and, finding it warm, guessed he had a fever. Immediately she tried to reduce the fever by keeping a cool, wet cloth on the baby's forehead, but the treatment didn't work. As the morning progressed Prem's fever became worse, and his mother was very worried. By lunchtime Prem's forehead was hot to the touch.

"I think Prem needs to see a doctor," Mother said.

"But Mother, there is no doctor in our village," Kamala said. "What will we do?"

It was a good question. There were no telephones in Kamala's village, and Kamala's family was too poor to own a car. There weren't even any buses or trains that passed through, and the nearest doctor was in another village almost five miles away—that is, if you followed the main road. There was, however, a shortcut through the jungle, but most people were afraid to take it because of tigers.

Mother put her hand on Kamala's shoulder. "Please go ask Mr. Gupta if you can borrow his bicycle. Tell him I'll cook his favorite supper for him if he lets you borrow it."

Kamala set off to find Mr. Gupta, but she had her doubts that he would lend her his bike. Mr. Gupta never shared anything he owned, including the fruit from his two big mango trees. If anyone even touched a fallen mango, Mr. Gupta would shout at them and shake his fist. Some people said that he acted that way because he was rich compared to everyone else—so rich that he didn't have to leave the village to find work. When he wasn't outside shouting and shaking his fists, Mr. Gupta sat in his house all day counting money. But he didn't share any of that money. Even the beggars knew not to bother Mr. Gupta.

Mr. Gupta lived by himself in the large house made out of concrete blocks, by far the grandest house in the village. The precious mango trees were in the front yard, and they were protected by a wire fence. Just as Kamala expected, they were full of ripe, juicy mangoes. But there were just as many mangoes lying on the ground, and these were beginning to rot and attract flies. Mangoes were Kamala's favorite fruit, and she wished that she could pick one off the tree. No wonder Mr. Gupta never needed to work, she thought. He had all the food he wanted in his own yard. He had too much.

At the gate Kamala took a deep breath and called out. "Mr. Gupta! Mr. Gupta!"

There was no answer from the house. *Maybe if I touch one of his precious mangoes,* she thought, *he'll come running out.* But she didn't want him shouting and shaking his fists, so she decided against it.

Kamala was relieved to see that the wire gate was unlocked. At least Mr. Gupta was at home. She took a deep breath, opened the gate, and stepped into the forbidden yard. Her legs felt like rubber, but she knew what had to be done.

At Mr. Gupta's front door some of her courage left her, and she knocked timidly. Nobody answered. After a few minutes Kamala forced herself to knock louder. *Think of Prem,* she reminded herself.

A sudden loud noise made her jump back.

"Yes?" It was Mr. Gupta.

Kamala trembled. "Sir, my bike is sick. May I borrow your brother to get the doctor?" she asked.

Mr. Gupta laughed. "I don't have a brother."

Kamala's face burned with embarrassment. "I mean," she said, "may I borrow your bicycle."

Mr. Gupta shook his head. "I never lend my bicycle— to anyone." He started to close the door.

"But, sir," Kamala said, "my brother is very sick. Would you go and get the doctor for us?"

Mr. Gupta looked annoyed. "I am a busy man, little girl. I don't have time to do errands for everybody."

Kamala wondered what it was that kept Mr. Gupta so busy—besides counting his money—but she didn't dare ask. "Sir, if you lend me your bicycle, I'll clean up all the fallen mangoes in your yard. I'll even pick the fresh ones off the tree and put them in baskets for you."

Mr. Gupta stared hard at Kamala, and it was all she could do to keep from running away. After a long time he shook his head again. "No. I've decided that my bicycle is too valuable to lend to you. What if you lost it, or it got stolen? No, I'll go get the doctor, myself. But I'll go later on this afternoon, when I'm ready. I was planning to go to that village anyway."

"But, sir, my brother needs the doctor now," Kamala said stubbornly.

Mr. Gupta closed the door in Kamala's face.

"You *are* the meanest man in India!" she shouted, and then ran all the way home. When she arrived she found that her brother was even sicker. It was clear that something had to be done immediately.

"There is that path that cuts across the edge of the jungle," Kamala reminded her mother. "If I follow that shortcut, it will take me only half as long to get to the doctor."

Mother was about to tell Kamala not to take the shortcut, but Prem began to shake violently. "I think he has malaria," Mother said.

"Please, Mother. Let me take the shortcut."

Mother glanced up at the sky. It was sunny and bright, and there was plenty of daylight left. "All right then, hurry. I'll pray for you. And stay in the middle of the path.''

Kamala walked so fast that she was almost running. She did this for Prem's sake, not her own. Kamala was not afraid to go into the jungle. She had been there many times with her father when he went to cut firewood. Kamala knew that if she minded her own business and kept to the path, the wild animals would probably not bother her.

The jungle was a very noisy place, full of bird and insect sounds. When Kamala entered it there seemed to be birds singing everywhere. One that Kamala especially liked sounded a lot like a flute.

''The birds are singing because they're happy,'' she told herself. ''And the birds are happy because there aren't any dangerous animals around. As long as the birds keep singing, I know there is nothing to worry about.'' The happy sound of the birds helped Kamala take her mind off Prem, and soon she was trying to imitate the flute bird.

Kamala had gone about a mile and was getting a little tired from her fast pace when suddenly the birds stopped singing. Kamala stopped dead in her tracks, but all she could hear was the pounding of her heart. She listened closely for a moment, but didn't hear any birds at all. Even the insects were silent.

Suddenly a huge orange tiger leaped out of some bushes and landed right in the middle of the path in front of her. It happened so quickly that Kamala didn't have time to scream.

Tigers are even bigger than lions, and this one was as tall as Kamala and about ten feet long. Its mouth was open and Kamala could see the long, pointed incisor teeth that tigers use to tear their victims apart. Tigers are supposed to have four of these teeth, but this tiger was missing one.

Kamala knew from the stories she had heard in her village that wounded tigers, or those missing teeth, often became man-eaters.

The tiger took a big step toward Kamala, and she could feel its warm breath on her face. It smelled like rotten meat. But Kamala was too scared to move. Her legs felt as though they were made of stone.

I am going to die, she thought. *I will never see my parents or Prem again.* She closed her eyes and prayed that the tiger would kill her quickly. She prayed that it wouldn't hurt very badly when he bit her. Above all, she didn't want to hear her own bones crunch.

Kamala waited and waited for the tiger to bite her, but nothing happened. She opened her eyes and couldn't believe what she saw. It had to be a dream. The tiger was lying down in the path at her feet. Its eyes and mouth were closed. Standing beside the tiger was a person in shining white clothes. Kamala couldn't tell if it was a man or a woman.

Kamala thought she was dreaming. "Who are you?" she asked the person in her dream.

"I'm an angel," the figure said. "I was sent here to protect you from the tiger."

"Is the tiger dead?" Kamala asked.

"It's sleeping," the angel said. "Now go back home. Your little brother will be all right. His fever is gone."

"Thank you. And thank you for saving my life," Kamala remembered to say.

The angel smiled. "I have saved your life many times before, Kamala. And I will do it again. Now hurry home to your mother and brother."

"What do you mean?" Kamala asked. She couldn't remember any other times when her life had been in danger. "And how do you know my name?"

But the angel had started to fade. In less than a minute it totally disappeared. In its place rays of sunshine streamed down through the trees to shine on the sleeping tiger.

Kamala realized with a jolt that she wasn't dreaming after all. She tested her legs. This time she could move them. She stepped soundlessly back a few steps and then turned around and ran. She believed that the angel would protect her, but she wasn't taking any chances. About a hundred feet down the path Kamala turned her head to see if the tiger was following her, but it was nowhere to be seen.

When Kamala got back to her house she found her mother smiling.

"Your little brother is going to be all right," Mother said. "His fever is gone."

"I know," Kamala said.

Her mother gave her a strange look. "Why are you back so soon? It takes longer than that to get to the doctor's. Even with the shortcut."

Kamala told her mother about the tiger and the angel. Her mother reached out and touched Kamala's forehead. "Maybe you have the fever now," she said. It was clear that she didn't believe Kamala.

Late that afternoon Mr. Gupta came by with a basket full of mangoes. He seemed relieved to see Kamala. He asked to speak to her alone, but Mother insisted on hearing what he had to say.

"I am not the meanest man in India," Mr. Gupta said. There was a twinkle in his eye, but Kamala didn't see it.

58

"I'm sorry I said that," she mumbled. But she wasn't sorry at all.

"Well, I'm sorry I didn't lend you my bicycle," he said, handing her the mangoes. "Is your brother all right?"

Kamala nodded. She didn't feel like being friendly to Mr. Gupta, even if he had brought mangoes.

"Good," Mr. Gupta said. "About an hour after you left I followed you on the jungle trail with my bicycle, but I couldn't catch up with you."

"That's because I turned around and came home."

"It's a good thing you did," Mr. Gupta said. "Halfway down the trail I came across tiger prints. They were the largest I've ever seen. If my hunch is right, they belong to a man-eater that has killed two people so far."

"Were they fresh prints?" asked Mother, giving Kamala a worried look.

"Very. In fact, by the marks in the dirt, I'd say that tiger decided to take an afternoon nap right there in the middle of the path."

"That's exactly what he did!" Kamala said. "I saw him sleeping beside the angel."

Mr. Gupta smiled. "Children have such wild imaginations," he told her mother. "Well, I have to get back to my house. When you're done with the mangoes, feel free to pick some more."

Kamala and her mother thanked Mr. Gupta for the fruit.

A week later Mr. Gupta showed up again with more mangoes. "You haven't been by to pick any," he said to Kamala. He almost sounded sad.

Kamala didn't know what to say. She still didn't trust the man.

"Well, never mind. Enjoy these," Mr. Gupta said, handing the basket to her. He started to leave, then stopped.

"Oh, I heard this morning that a hunter shot the man-eater yesterday. Unfortunately, it had just killed its third victim."

Kamala shuddered. "Did it have only three big teeth?" she asked.

Mr. Gupta stared at her in surprise. "How did you know?"

"Because it was the one that would have killed me, if it hadn't been for my guardian angel," she said matter-of-factly.

Mr. Gupta shook his head. "Children and their imaginations!" he said. He was smiling.

Maria's Angel

*But as he was sleeping, an angel touched him and
told him to get up and eat.*

—I Kings 19:5

Maria was sound asleep in her family's apartment
in Mexico City when the earthquake hit. She was
dreaming that she was riding a bumpy roller coaster, when
suddenly she was thrown out of bed and onto the hard,
cold floor. Maria realized at once that it was an earthquake.

"Mama!" she screamed. "Papa!"

Maria stood up. It was like standing on a trampoline.
She tried taking a few steps toward her bedroom door, but
the floor was shaking so hard that she lost her balance
and fell backward, hitting her head on the edge of the bed.
Maria was so dizzy then that all she could do was crawl
under her bed for protection. Even though the earthquake
was still going on, she fell right back to sleep.

When Maria woke up the earthquake had stopped, but
the air was full of dust. She was lying on her stomach,
with her face pressed against the floor. Even under the

bed it was so dusty that she could hardly breathe. Maria pulled her pajama top up over her mouth and nose to help keep the dust out, then she fell back to sleep.

The third time she woke up the dust had settled. Maria was wide-awake now, but she had the worst headache of her life. Even if she moved just a little it hurt so much that she had to stop.

"Mama!" she yelled. "Papa!" It felt as if a hammer was hitting her head.

The only way to keep her head from hurting was to lie absolutely still and remain silent. But Maria could not silence her thoughts. It was pitch-black under the bed, and the darkness frightened her. *Maybe I'm dead,* she thought. *Maybe I'm not under my bed, but in a grave. But I can't be dead because my head hurts, and dead people don't feel pain. No, I'm alive and in my bedroom. This is my bed above me. I know it is, even though I can't see it.*

Suddenly it occurred to Maria that her mother and father, and her older brother Jose, might all have been killed by the earthquake.

"Dear God," she prayed silently, "please don't let Mama and Papa be dead. Even Jose," she added. "And please, God, help me. Please!" she pleaded.

After a while, even though her head felt as though it was going to burst, Maria forced herself to move. Inch by painful inch she scooted to the side of the bed nearest the door. She was very careful not to bump her head against the bottom of the mattress. When she thought she had reached the edge, she reached out into the blackness with her fingers. They bumped against plaster and boards. The ceiling had fallen and was blocking her way.

Maria lay very still for a long time. She listened hard for the sound of people coming to her rescue, but the only thing she heard was the beating of her heart. To calm herself, Maria tried thinking about all the things that bored her the most—like arithmetic.

Eventually Maria fell asleep and dreamed about angels. In her dream an angel appeared to her in a circle of light. The angel was named Celeste, and was Maria's own special guardian angel. The angel told Maria that she would be all right, and that Maria could help her situation by listening to her own inner voice.

When she woke up the fourth time her headache was gone. *Maybe I'm dead now,* she thought with horror. She dug a fingernail into her thumb to see if it hurt. It did, and she breathed a sigh of relief.

"Mama!" she called. "Papa!" It no longer hurt to yell, but still there was no answer.

Suddenly Maria felt an urge to move to the other side of the bed. Maybe the ceiling hadn't fallen there. It would feel so good just to sit up for a change. Carefully and slowly Maria turned her face in the other direction. That's when she saw the moving light at the edge of the bed.

"Mama! Papa! Anybody! I'm here, under the bed."

Nobody answered. Moving just an inch at a time, so as not to get her headache back, Maria began to scoot over to the side of the bed where the light was.

The light moved away from the edge of the bed and lit up a small part of her bedroom on that side. Maria could see that the ceiling had fallen down there too, but a couple of the big wooden beams had landed at an angle, forming a space like a small tent.

Maria pulled herself out from underneath the bed and into the space. It wasn't high enough for her to stand, but at least she could sit up. It felt like heaven to sit.

Maria looked around to see where the light was coming

from, and then realized that she was sitting in it. It wasn't a bright light and it wasn't in any one spot. It was a dim, fuzzy light, just bright enough for Maria to see her hands and her feet.

This is my angel, she thought. *My angel is right here all around me.* Then, even though she felt silly doing it, Maria spoke aloud.

"Hello, guardian angel. Can you hear me?"

"Of course I can hear you," Celeste said. To Maria, Celeste's voice was like thoughts, but much stronger thoughts than any she had ever had. It was as if Celeste was speaking in her head.

"Thank you, God," Maria said.

"Yes," Celeste agreed. "We must definitely thank God."

Suddenly Maria realized that she was very, very thirsty. "Please, Celeste," she said, "give me something to drink."

Then Maria felt very silly. What was there to drink in a little space beneath two fallen beams? Did she expect Celeste to just hand her a glass of water, or maybe a milk shake?

"That wasn't a silly question at all," Celeste said firmly.

Maria was shocked. "Can you read my mind, Celeste?"

Celeste laughed, and to Maria it felt almost like hiccups. "No, I can't read your mind. Not if you don't want me to. But right now, we're talking in your mind, remember?"

"Yes, of course. Now, how about that water?"

The light in the little space beneath the beams got brighter for a few seconds. When it dimmed, Maria could feel Celeste talking again. "Over there, in the corner, just behind the second beam. Reach back in there."

Maria was still not a hundred percent convinced that her angel Celeste was real, but just to be on the safe side she crawled over to the far end of the space and reached back behind the second beam. At first all she could feel were sharp pieces of broken plaster, and something that felt like a sweatshirt. But when her fingers closed around a smooth, plastic object, Maria knew exactly what it was.

"My drinking bottle from soccer practice!" she cried joyfully and pulled it out into the open.

There were still about three inches of water in the bottle, and even though it was warm and tasted like plastic, to Maria it was the best drink she had ever had.

"Hold on," Celeste said. "You need to make that last."

Maria felt as though she had just swallowed a brick. "You mean I'm not going to be rescued right away?"

"Not right away. But soon."

"How soon?"

"Tomorrow. Tomorrow afternoon."

Maria screwed the top back onto the plastic bottle and set it down carefully. "I'm not going to like having to spend the night trapped here like a prisoner."

"You've already spent two nights here," Celeste said gently.

"But that can't be!" exclaimed Maria. "It didn't seem like two nights."

"You hit your head very hard," Celeste said. "I suppose I'm to blame for that."

"You?"

When Celeste sighed it felt like a trickle to Maria. "I tried to wake you up in your dream. You know, the roller coaster dream. But you liked that dream, and didn't want to wake up. I should have tried a scarier dream."

"No, you did your best," Maria said generously. She

65

was beginning to think of Celeste as a very special friend. Then something occurred to her. "Hey, you helped me find water. Now, how about some food?"

"I was afraid you'd think of that." Celeste sounded more concerned than annoyed. 'I'm not a restaurant, you know."

"Just a little something?" Maria asked. "I'm awfully hungry."

It seemed like Celeste had to think for a while. "Okay," she said at last, "but it isn't much."

"Whatever it is, it'll be just fine," Maria assured her.

"Then reach back into that corner and pull out the sweatshirt you felt. There's something in the left pocket."

Maria couldn't remember leaving anything to eat in any of her pockets. She was always hungry, especially when she played soccer. And that was usually when she wore that sweatshirt. Still, something was better than nothing, so she obeyed Celeste and retrieved the old sweatshirt.

"Hey, there's nothing but these," she said, pulling out a couple of breath mints that were wadded up in some foil.

"Well, I didn't promise you a feast," Celeste said. "You could be thankful for what you have."

Maria could tell that she had hurt Celeste's feelings. "I'm sorry, really. I *am* thankful. It's just that I'm so hungry."

Celeste seemed content with Maria's apology. "Now get some sleep. You need it to get better, and it will help pass the time faster."

Maria thought that made sense. "But where will you be when I'm sleeping? Will you stay here with me?"

"Now that *is* silly," Celeste said. "Of course I'll stay here with you. I am your guardian angel, aren't I?"

"Are you always with me?" Maria asked. "And if so,

how come I've never been able to speak to you until now?''

This time Maria felt a shiver run through her body when Celeste answered. "I was assigned to you before you were even born, Maria. I was with you that time you had the tricycle accident when you were three. Who do you think it was that made that car swerve so that it didn't hit you?''

"That was you?''

"Well it wasn't the wind!''

"Sorry, again,'' Maria said. She would try harder not to hurt Celeste's feelings.

"I work very hard, you know.''

"I'm sure you do. Will you be with me the rest of my life? Even when I'm grown-up?'' Maria had heard of children having guardian angels, but not adults.

"Of course,'' Celeste assured her. "But when you're grown-up it might be harder to hear me. That's why adults don't think they have guardian angels. Because they can't hear us like you do.''

"But I never heard you before the earthquake,'' Maria pointed out.

"Sure you did. You didn't hear me as clearly as you do now, but you heard me deep inside. Whenever you had a feeling that you shouldn't do something bad—''

"That was you?'' Maria interrupted her.

"Most of the time. Anyway, Maria, tomorrow when you wake up you won't hear me this clearly again. I only speak this loud and clear when someone is in serious danger.''

The thought that Celeste's voice would fade away made Maria very sad. "Then how will I know that you were real, and that this wasn't all a dream?'' she demanded.

"Would it matter so much if it was a dream?'' Celeste asked.

"Yes," Maria said, "it would. If I knew it wasn't a dream, then I would know I could count on you in the future."

"You'll know," Celeste assured her.

"But how?"

There was no answer from Celeste and the light in the space grew gradually dimmer, but it did not disappear altogether. Maria began to doubt that her angel had ever existed. If it hadn't been for the dim light that still lit up the space under the beams, she would have been very much afraid again.

After a while Maria fell asleep. When she woke up the space was brightly lit.

"Oh, Celeste! You're back!" Maria exclaimed.

It wasn't Celeste that answered but the sound of a noisy jackhammer. Maria had seen workmen use them to tear up big hunks of the street. Dust began to pour down into her little space and Maria had to cover her nose and mouth again in order to breath.

Then the noisy jackhammer stopped and Maria heard voices. Men's voices.

"I think I see one," a deep voice said.

"Help!" Maria shouted. She shouted as loudly as she could, but it was barely a squeak.

"A live one!" the man said.

There was more dust, and the beams above her creaked. Then a pair of strong hands reached down and picked her up and pulled through a hole at the top of the space.

Maria was rushed to the hospital, where the doctors examined her carefully. Except for the fact that she needed food and water, there was nothing wrong. Even the bump on the back of her head had disappeared. In a few days she was as good as new. Everyone agreed that it was a miracle that Maria had survived three days under all that rubble and was in such good condition.

Maria's family was not so lucky. Her brother Jose had a broken arm, and her parents were badly hurt. They had to stay in the hospital for almost a month.

When her parents got better Maria told them the story about Celeste, and how she had helped her following the earthquake. Fortunately, Maria's parents believed her. Jose did not. He loved to tease Maria about Celeste.

"Does your precious angel have wings?" Jose asked one day.

"No," Maria said. "I mean, I didn't see any wings, because I didn't actually see her."

"Then how do you know she was an angel? Maybe she was a ghost?"

"But—"

"Or even an alien?"

"She told me she was an angel," Maria said stubbornly.

"You're crazy, you know that?"

Maria started to cry.

"Crybaby, crybaby!" Jose taunted. "Cry—" He stopped, and a strange expression came over his face.

"What's the matter?" Maria asked as she wiped her face. Jose's eyes had gotten very big and seemed to be looking at something beside her. His mouth kept opening and closing, but no sound came out.

Maria glanced quickly around, but saw nothing unusual. "What's wrong?" she asked. She loved her big brother, and it was easy for her to forgive him.

"I—I—I see Celeste," Jose stammered.

Maria felt tricked. "Quit making fun of me," she cried. "I really did see my angel."

"But I'm not making fun of you. Honest. She's gone

69

now, but for a minute I saw someone standing beside you. I think it was your angel, Celeste.''

"What did she look like?'' asked Maria eagerly.

"It's hard to say exactly. She was mostly light. You know, sort of a shape made out of light.''

"Then it was Celeste!''

"I guess it had to be,'' Jose said. His face was serious.

Maria couldn't help herself. "Did Celeste have wings?'' she asked.

Jose didn't even smile. "No, no wings. But a definite shape—like a person.''

A tingle ran up Maria's spine. In a way Celeste had come to her rescue again. She wished that she had seen a definite shape as well, but at least she had heard Celeste speak.

Sometimes when Maria is very quiet Celeste still speaks to her. It is a very soft voice, more like thoughts in her head, but Maria knows it is Celeste. And since that day when Jose saw Celeste standing next to his sister, he has not teased her about angels.

Dana's Angel

"... The angel who has delivered me from all harm ..."

—*Genesis 48:16*

Uncle Frank had to be the world's worst driver. He was in three car accidents in one year, and each of them had been his fault. On top of that, he had five tickets for reckless driving.

"The police should just take away his license," Mrs. Katz said about her younger brother.

"But it's fun to ride with Uncle Frank," Don said.

"You'd better not ride with Uncle Frank, anymore," warned Mother. "If I catch you riding with him again, I'll ground you for a week, *and* keep your allowance."

Don made a face at his twin sister, Dana. "You told on me, huh?"

"Well, it was for your own good," Dana said. She didn't always get along with her twin, but she loved him and didn't want him to get hurt, or possibly even killed.

"Tell on me again and you'll be sorry," Don whispered.

"What was that?" Mother demanded.

"Nothing," Don muttered.

Dana shrugged. "Can I go now? I have to draw a map of New Jersey for school."

Mother sighed. "Okay. I guess the lecture is over—for this time. But no more riding with Uncle Frank, get it?"

"Got it," Don said. He made another face at his sister as soon as Mother wasn't looking.

The next day it was raining as the twins walked home from school. Because the day had started out sunny, neither of them had thought to bring an umbrella. Dana held her notebook above her head to keep the rain off her, but Don liked getting wet. He especially liked jumping in puddles and splashing his sister.

"Stop it!" Dana said for the millionth time.

"What's the matter? Afraid you're going to melt?"

Just then Uncle Frank pulled up beside them in his dented car. "Want a ride?" he called out to them.

"No thanks," Dana said. "It's not that far."

"She means she's chicken," Don said.

"Am not!"

"You are so." Don started clucking like a hen.

"Just because I don't want to be in an accident, doesn't mean I'm a chicken," Dana told her twin.

Uncle Frank looked as though his feelings were hurt. "Hey, I was just offering you guys a ride, that's all."

"Mother said—" Dana began, and then stopped. She knew Uncle Frank didn't like hearing what his older sister had to say about his bad driving habits.

"Yeah?" Uncle Frank said. "What did my sister say?"

"Nothing," Don said, climbing into the front seat beside his uncle. "You coming, or are you going to be a chicken tattletale again?" he asked Dana.

Dana didn't want to hurt her uncle's feelings, and she didn't like being called "chicken." But most of all she didn't like getting wet. She had gotten an "A" on her map of New Jersey, and even though it was safely tucked inside her notebook, it was probably already ruined.

"I'll come along this one time," she said, "but next time we have to walk."

"Yeah, yeah," Don said, buckling his seat belt.

"Hop in," Uncle Frank said. "The backseat is all yours."

Dana had never been in her uncle's car. It was even crummier than she had imagined, but at least it was dry. "Where's the seat belt?" she asked.

"Aren't any in back," Uncle Frank said.

He stepped on the gas and the car shot away from the curb like a bullet. Almost immediately he made a sharp right turn on High Street and Dana was thrown against the side of the car. She barely had time to brace herself before her uncle made another sharp turn onto Broadmore Avenue. The tires screeched loudly.

"Yahoo!" Don shouted. "This is fun!"

"You ain't seen nothing yet," laughed Uncle Frank. He made such a sharp turn on Oak Street that even though she was braced, Dana was thrown against the side of the car again.

Suddenly a police car appeared out of nowhere with its siren wailing.

"Oh, oh," Don said. He slid down as far as his seat belt would allow him.

Uncle Frank swore, but he kept right on driving. In fact, he sped up.

"Aren't you going to stop?" Dana yelled. The police car was right behind them and the siren was deafening.

"Can't," shouted Uncle Frank. "If I do, they'll take away my license. Hold on!"

Dana held on, but it was hard not to get thrown around. Riding in the back of Uncle Frank's car was like riding in the last car of the big roller coaster at the amusement park. It was certainly more frightening than that. At least at the amusement park you knew you would arrive safely at the end of the ride.

Dana closed her eyes. "Dear God," she prayed, "please don't let me get killed. Or Don, either. Or even Uncle Frank."

For the next few minutes they twisted and jerked around corners at top speed. The sound of honking horns and screeching tires told Dana that they had driven through several red lights. She continued to pray.

Now Dana could hear two police sirens, but still Uncle Frank refused to stop. "Don't worry, they can't catch me!" he shouted.

Just then a third siren added to the noise, and Dana knew deep down inside that something terrible was about to happen. She was right. A second later they were on the Becker Street overpass with a police car right on their tail. At the same time two police cars were coming straight at them from the other direction. Uncle Frank slammed on the brakes. The car bucked like a wild horse. It seemed to have a life of its own. The steering wheel was jerked out of Uncle Frank's hands and the car went crashing through the guardrail. As it fell to the street below it flipped over from front to back, ending upside down on the hard pavement.

It felt like slow motion to Dana when Uncle Frank's car left the pavement and went flying into the air off the side of the Becker Street overpass. *I'm not even wearing a seat belt, so I'm going to die,* she thought. *I don't want to die. The funny thing is, I'm not even scared. I'm mad! I'm mad at Uncle Frank for driving like a crazy fool. And I'm mad at Don for daring me to ride with Uncle Frank. I guess I'm even mad at myself for listening to them. Now I'm never going to see Mother and Dad again. Or my grandparents. Or my best friend, Susan. What an idiot I am for not obeying Mother.*

She closed her eyes, ready to die. "Please, God, don't let it hurt too bad," she prayed.

Suddenly Dana felt very calm. She could no longer hear the sirens. It was the most peaceful feeling she had ever known. She opened her eyes and what she saw made her think she was already dead, because there was an angel on either side of her. Then she realized that she was still in the car, not in heaven, and that the angels were holding her gently in their arms.

Dana could hear the crash, but she could not feel it when the car smashed on the street below. Her angels kept her from feeling any of the impact, and they very gently put her down on the ceiling of the upside-down car. Then just as suddenly as they had arrived, the angels disappeared, vanishing into thin air.

The slow motion sped up and Dana could hear sirens again. She could also hear moans from the front seat, where Don was. Uncle Frank was silent. Too silent, thought Dana. Maybe dead silent.

The weight of the car had flattened its roof and Dana could not see up into the front seat area. She tried to open the back door of the car, but it wouldn't open. The space Dana was in was so small she couldn't imagine how two angels had fitted in there with her, but somehow they had.

The firemen had to help the police get the twins and

Uncle Frank out of the car. They had to cut the sides of the car open with blowtorches and it took them over an hour. When they finally got them out they rushed them all to the hospital in ambulances, including Dana.

"But I'm all right," Dana kept insisting.

And she was, although nobody could quite believe it.

"It's the most incredible thing I've ever seen," said one of the firemen who had helped rescue her. "I just can't understand how a car could get crushed so bad, and yet somebody survived without a scratch. And she wasn't even wearing a seat belt!"

"That's because two angels held me in," Dana told everyone who would listen.

But much to her dismay, nobody believed her, not even Mother. Even her minister said that there had to be another reason she wasn't hurt, a reason no one had thought of yet.

Fortunately Don and Uncle Frank both survived the accident as well. Don was in the hospital for several days, but Uncle Frank had to stay in for much longer than that. First they put him in an intensive care unit, where he wasn't allowed any visitors except his parents. He had to stay in there for almost a month.

Finally when they moved him to a regular hospital room the twins were allowed to visit him. Mother had told them not to talk about the accident because it might upset their uncle, but Uncle Frank wanted to talk about it.

"I'm very sorry for what I did," he said. "Will you two forgive me?"

"Yes," Dana said. She didn't feel angry at her uncle anymore. She just hoped that he had learned his lesson.

"How about you, Don?" their uncle asked.

Don shrugged. "You know, I broke my arm and had to drop out of Little League?"

"Sorry again," Uncle Frank said.

"It's all right."

"I hear you weren't hurt at all," Uncle Frank said to Dana.

"Some people have all the luck," Don grumbled.

"It wasn't luck," Dana said.

"What do you mean?" Uncle Frank asked.

"She says that angels protected her," Don said. "Like they were seat belts. Can you believe that?" He laughed.

Uncle Frank stared at them with his mouth open. "Actually, I can," he said after a long pause.

"What?" Don could hardly believe his ears. Uncle Frank was no fool, even if he was a terrible driver.

"I saw the angels," Uncle Frank said quietly.

"Come on! You've got to be kidding," Don said.

"No, I'm not kidding. Just as the car went off the bridge I looked in the rearview mirror because I was worried about Dana. I was feeling guilty for having made her take a ride she didn't want to take."

"You didn't make me do anything," Dana said quickly. "I could have walked home in the rain. It was my choice."

Uncle Frank smiled at her. "You're an angel yourself, you know that? Anyway, when I looked in the mirror I saw two angels, one on either side of you, and they were holding you in their arms. Then the next thing I knew I was here in the hospital. I guess I'd been here a long time before I came to."

"Wow!" Don said. He could feel the hair on his arms standing on end.

Dana started to cry, but they were tears of joy. "I'm so glad you saw the angels too, Uncle Frank. I know what I saw, but I was beginning to think maybe I had just dreamed it. You see, even my minister thought it must have been a dream.''

"Definitely not," Uncle Frank assured her. "Unless we had the same dream.''

They all laughed. And although it shouldn't have made a difference, from then on Don treated his twin sister a lot better. Well, most of the time.

Jakob's Angel

*That night, when he stopped to camp at sundown, he
... dreamed that a staircase reached from earth to
heaven, and he saw the angels of God going up and
down upon it.*

—Genesis 28:11–12

*I*t was sunset when Jakob and his little brother David found
the perfect place to hide from the Nazis. The brothers
were Jewish, and had been running and hiding from the
Nazis ever since the German army invaded their tiny town
on the Polish border. All the Jews in their hometown were
eventually rounded up and sent off to concentration camps.
That is, all the Jews except for Jakob and David.

Thanks to their mother, the boys had been sent away before the Nazis arrived. Mrs. Bronski had had a dream in
which an angel told her to send her sons to the home of a
woodcutter who lived in the forest. Mrs. Bronski knew the
woodcutter because she often bought wood from him when
he was in town. The day after her dream, Mrs. Bronski made
arrangements to have the boys stay with the woodcutter and

his wife for a long time. She paid them a lot of money and they promised to take good care of the boys.

But when the Nazis invaded Poland the woodcutter became nervous about hiding two Jewish boys and told them they had to leave. The boys would have returned home, and most likely would have been sent to a concentration camp, too, except that the woodcutter's wife felt sorry for them.

"Here, take this food," she said, handing them a small cloth bundle that contained a loaf of bread and some cheese. "But don't go back home yet. The Germans are still in your town. Maybe you should hide someplace in this forest until they're gone." She patted them both on the head. "But hide a long way from here," she added. She liked the boys, but didn't want the Nazis to find out that she had been hiding Jews.

The boys hid in the roots of a large overturned tree on the banks of a stream for five days. During that time they ate all the bread and cheese, plus some nuts and wild berries they found growing near their hiding place. They began to get very hungry.

"I want to go home," David said.

"So do I, but we can't. Not until the Germans leave."

"When will that be?"

Jakob kicked softly at one of the tree roots. "I don't know. Maybe never."

David began to cry.

"Sssh!" Jakob said. "The Nazis might hear you."

"I don't care," David wailed. "I'm hungry!"

"Then we have to leave this place," Jakob said, "and find someplace where nobody knows we're Jewish. Then we'll beg for food."

Little David didn't care what his brother's plans were, as long as they included food.

The next morning the brothers started walking even deeper into the forest, leaving their little town and the woodcutter's house far behind. Soon they were completely lost. That night they slept under an overhanging rock and covered themselves with fallen leaves to keep warm.

The following morning they began walking again, but very slowly, because they were weak from hunger. After a few hours David couldn't walk any farther and so Jakob carried him on his back. After that Jakob had to stop and rest many times, but hunger kept him going again as long as he possibly could. Near sunset the boys found themselves at the edge of the woods.

"Look," Jakob said. He put his brother down and pointed off to the horizon.

David could just barely see a large country house surrounded by spacious lawns. There was smoke rising from the chimney. Behind the house was a small barn, which undoubtedly held chickens and cows to supply eggs and milk to the owners. "Is that our new home?" he asked.

Jakob smiled. "For tonight, at least. I have an idea."

Jakob's idea was to wait until dark. Then he and his brother would sneak onto the estate and hide in the barn.

After darkness had fallen the boys set out for the farm. This time David walked. The sight of the farmhouse and the possibility of getting food had made him stronger.

But Jakob had no intention of stopping at the farmhouse. There was always a chance that the farmer and his wife didn't like Jews and would turn them away. Or worse yet, turn them over to the Nazis. Sticking to the deep shadows, Jakob led his little brother past the house and to the barn. The door was closed, but it wasn't locked.

Jakob was glad that there were no dogs on this farm. He liked dogs, but dogs would bark and bring the farmer or his wife out to investigate. It was bad enough that when the boys sneaked into the barn some chickens began to squawk. The boys froze, holding their breath, and soon the chickens settled down. There was very little light to see by in the barn, and Jakob carefully steered David over to what looked like a pile of hay. They were just a few feet from the hay pile when suddenly it stood up and began to moo. Jakob clamped his hand over David's mouth to keep him from screaming.

Jakob stood stock-still, waiting for his eyes to adjust in the gloom. When they did, he noticed a real hay pile in the far corner away from the cow. He gave his brother a gentle push. "Go hide in there. Up to your neck. If anybody comes, pull the hay up over your face."

The little boy was still terrified. "Where are you going?"

"To get food," Jakob said. "Rich people live in that house. There has to be something to eat around here. If I can't find anything, then I'll have to milk the cow. But I don't know how," he added miserably.

David obediently hid in the scratchy hay pile while his brother searched for food. *What if the farmer or his wife comes into the barn and finds me here?* he worried. *What if they catch Jakob and leave me all alone? What will I do?* He sobbed softly, and the cow mooed softly as if in response.

After what seemed like hours Jakob returned. This time the chickens stayed silent.

"Look what I found," Jakob said happily. "And I have a whole bunch of them." He handed his brother something small and round.

"What is it?" David asked sleepily.

"A potato!"

"But it's raw."

"Beggars can't be choosers," Jakob said and he wiped a potato clean on his shirt before biting into it. It was the best food he had ever tasted.

That night the boys slept well in the warm hay. When Jakob woke up the sun was shining. At once he realized that they had overslept.

"Come on." He poked his sleeping brother. "We've got to get back to the woods before anyone sees us."

"I already see you," someone said.

Jakob sat bolt upright. His heart pounded so hard he thought it might burst through the walls of his chest. A teenage girl was standing above them with a milk bucket in her hand.

"I'm s-sorry—"

The girl smiled pleasantly. "You're Jewish children, aren't you?"

"I am," said Jakob, "but my brother isn't." Then he realized how silly that had sounded. "I meant to say my friend, not my brother."

The girl's smile was even bigger. "It's all right. You're safe with me." She reached out her hand to help him up from the hay, but Jakob still wasn't sure if he could trust her.

"I think you should have some breakfast," the girl said. "Don't you?"

"Breakfast?" Little David had awakened and had heard that tempting word.

"Yes, breakfast. Let's see, how do some eggs and toast sound? With homemade raspberry jam. And of course a big glass of milk." She pointed to the cow who was standing up, and in the daylight, didn't look anything like a pile of hay.

"That sounds wonderful," David said. He looked at his brother, but Jakob didn't seem very eager to accept the offer.

"Look, my name is Anna. Anna Jablonski. I work for

the owner and his wife, but they've gone into town and won't be back until after church. So it's safe for you to come out and have a good breakfast.''

The boys climbed out of the hay pile, but Jakob was determined not to trust her too soon. ''Thanks, but we have to be going as well.''

''But I want breakfast!'' David began to cry.

''Hush,'' Jakob said sternly. ''Don't be such a big baby. What if it's a trick?'' He turned to the girl. ''Who are you really, and why should we trust you?''

She tapped the bucket. ''I work here, and you can trust me because I say so.''

''You could be lying.''

The girl shrugged. ''Okay, have it your way. But I tried to help you, remember that.''

Jakob studied her face. It's hard to tell by someone's face if they are honest, but this face certainly looked honest. ''What is the owner's name?'' he asked.

''Andre Pavolitch,'' the girl answered.

Jakob's heart began to pound again. Andre Pavolitch was a banker and the owner of his town's newspaper. Everyone knew that Mr. Pavolitch hated Jews almost as much as the Nazis did. If he knew Jakob and his brother were hiding in the barn, he would turn them in at once.

The girl saw the frightened look on his face. ''Relax! My master will be gone for another two hours. By that time you can have had your breakfast and be well on your way. You will be all right, I promise. After all, you are very lucky children to have so many guardian angels.''

Jakob stared at her. ''What do you mean?''

The girl laughed, and then noticing that his expression hadn't changed, hurried to explain. ''Last night the Pavolitches were having a little too much wine with their supper. Mrs. Pavolitch thought she heard a noise coming from the barn—sometimes foxes do get in, you know—and she made Mr. Pavolitch go and see what the problem was. In a minute he was back, his face as white as a sheet.

" 'Well,' asked Mrs. Pavolitch, 'what is it?'

" 'I saw angels,' Mr. Pavolitch said. 'A band of them, standing shoulder to shoulder, surrounding the barn. And each of them was holding a flaming sword.'

"Well, Mrs. Pavolitch thought her husband was drunk and made him go off to bed without even finishing his supper. But first she made him promise to go to church this morning. They don't go to church every Sunday, you know.'' She laughed. ''But Mr. Pavolitch wasn't drunk last night, after all.''

''What do you mean?'' Jakob asked.

Anna's face became very serious. ''There really were angels surrounding the barn. I saw them myself, and I hadn't been drinking at all.''

Jakob grabbed his brother's hand. ''You're teasing us,'' he said. ''We'll be going now.''

''No!'' Anna cried, stepping in front of them with the bucket. ''I'm telling you the truth. I heard what Mr. Pavolitch told his wife, and I looked out the kitchen window and there they were!''

''Angels with flaming swords?'' Jakob asked. It sounded crazy to him.

Anna nodded. ''Well, I didn't see the swords. And I didn't see the angels. Not really. But when I looked out the window, at first I thought the barn was on fire. I mean, there was such a bright light around the barn, that it was all I could see.''

''And then?''

''And then Mrs. Pavolitch made me help her take Mr.

Pavolitch upstairs. She was afraid he would fall because he was drunk. But, of course he wasn't. When I got a chance to look out the window again all I could see was the barn—looking like it does right now.''

"Are you *sure* you didn't have anything to drink?'' Jakob asked.

Anna laughed again. "I'm sure. Nothing except milk. And speaking of which, we'd better get you some breakfast and on your way before the Pavolitches get back from church. Unless you want to trust your angels again.''

Jakob didn't know what to believe about the angels, but he did know that the smartest thing was to get as far away from the Pavolitches' house as possible before they returned. "Breakfast sounds great,'' he said, and helped David gather eggs, while Anna milked the cow.

After breakfast Anna sent them on their way with a sack full of bread, sausage, and hard-boiled eggs. She also gave them the address of a cousin of hers who lived in the next town and who would help them find a safe place to stay.

The brothers never saw their parents again, but they themselves survived until the end of the war, when it was safe for Jews to come out of hiding. They are grown men now, but they have never forgotten the kindness of Anna and her cousin, and many others like them. And even though they are still not quite sure what to believe, Anna's story about the angels is very special to them.